# Something Funny

# Happened at the Library

## How to Create Humorous Programs for Children and Young Adults

## Rob Reid

**American Library Association**
Chicago
2003

Project editor, Eloise L. Kinney

Composition by ALA Editions in Tekton and Berkeley using QuarkXPress 4.1 on a PC platform

Printed on 50-pound white offset, a pH-neutral stock, and bound in 10-point coated cover stock by Victor Graphics

The paper used in this publication meets the minimum requirements of American National Standard for Information Sciences—Permanence of Paper for Printed Library Materials, ANSI Z39.48-1992. ∞

**Library of Congress Cataloging-in-Publication Data**

Reid, Rob
    Something funny happened at the library : how to create humorous programs for children and young adults / by Rob Reid.
      p. cm.
    Includes bibliographical references and index.
    ISBN 0-8389-0836-5
    1. Children's libraries—Activity programs. 2. Young adults libraries—Activity programs. 3. Storytelling. I. Title.
Z718.1.R34 2002
027.62'5—dc21
                                       2002008970

Printed in the United States of America.

07   06   05   04   03      5   4   3   2   1

*Dedicated to Jayne—*
*Who, upon hearing that I had*
*the basic "stuff" in the computer*
*and now needed to find*
*a voice for the book, replied,*
*"How about Donald Duck's?"*

# Contents

# Acknowledgments

Thanks to Woody Allen, Dave Barry, John Belushi, Robert Benchley, Bob and Ray, Carol Burnett, *Cheers,* Michael Feldman, Jeff Foxworthy, Firesign Theatre, Garrison Keillor, Gary Larson, Laurel and Hardy, David Letterman, *Mad* magazine, the Marx Brothers, Monty Python, *Mystery Science Theatre 3000, The Onion,* Helen and Eldo Reid, Charles Schulz, Second City, the Smothers Brothers, James Thurber, Bill Waterson, Robin Williams, and Steven Wright for shaping my humor.

Thanks to Laura, Julia, Alice, and Sam.

And thanks to the thousands of kids throughout the years for laughing.

## PERMISSIONS

The author gratefully acknowledges permission to use the following: "Answering Machine Messages" by Ann Shuda; "Hippo Hop Hokey Pokey" by Kati Tvruska; "The Stinky Cheese Man Song" by Krista Falteisek; *The Web Files* by Margie Palatini.

# Introduction

*"Dying is easy. Comedy is hard."*

—Attributed to many sources

My job is to make kids laugh.

As a teacher, storyteller, writer, actor, neighbor, and father, I try to make kids laugh to get their attention. I try to make them laugh to make them feel good about themselves. I try to make them laugh because it's the best way I know to make a connection with folks who are many years younger than I. As a librarian, I try to make kids laugh for all these reasons, but also to ensure that they'll make a positive connection with the library—hopefully, one they'll have all their lives.

There are many research studies that show the benefits of humor in our busy lives. This is not one of them. This guide, which is aimed at both the experienced humorist and the many folks who tell me they're not naturally funny, is designed to share my favorite humor strategies and resources. It focuses on three aspects of humor for youth services librarians: tricks of the trade, programming models, and select bibliographies of humor books.

C'mon. Let's dive right into the good stuff. And if things go accordingly, you'll have the library director, city hall, the county board, and other area residents talking about all that loud laughter in the library.

# 1

## Tricks of the Trade

You don't have to be a natural at telling jokes or a former class clown to make children laugh. You don't need to dress up in a costume, stand on your head, juggle, or spin plates on sticks. Anyone can be funny by selecting the right material and knowing a few simple tricks of the trade.

### PREPARE YOUR AUDIENCE

When dealing with younger children, I let them know that they're in for a funny time even before the last audience member has entered the story area. Try out a line, such as "Whatever you do today—*don't laugh!*" That will start the giggles. Make small talk with the early arrivals, thus entertaining them and setting a light mood. Tell them, "I can't decide whether to read really funny stories today or sad, boring stories." They'll quickly vote for the funny stories, chuckling as they give you their feedback. Sometimes I'll ask the kids what stories they're going to read to me today. They'll usually smile and respond that I'm supposed to be the one reading stories. I'll react in mock horror that I didn't prepare anything and that we might have to simply stare at each other for the whole program. I'll then point to the stack of books in the story area and say, "I sure hope some of those are funny!" The kids are now primed for laughter.

When visiting a school or sponsoring a tour at the library, I'll sometimes set the mood by mixing up the students' ages. For example, I'll say to the kindergartners or first graders, "You must be the tenth-grade class." They'll quickly set me straight and, once again, the mood has been established for silliness.

My favorite technique for all audience age groups is to lead them through a series of "storyteller warm-ups." Here's how it goes:

"Please rise for the Official Storyteller Warm-Ups.

Since some of the stories and songs need the audience's help, I want to be sure that you're all properly warmed up.

We'll start by going through our vowels together.

Everyone, please give me a nice, quiet 'A.'"
> (*The audience says a long 'A'*)

"Now stretch out your lips for 'E-e-e-e.'"
> (*Pull your mouth wide open at the sides*)

"Give me a high 'I.'"
> (*Done in a falsetto voice*)

"Now a low 'O.'"
> (*Deep voice*)

"Now a 'U, U, U.'"
> (*Exaggerate your lips by pushing them forward*)

"Stretch your jaw muscles this way"
> (*Cup chin in one hand and turn head to one side*)

"and that way."
> (*Turn head in opposite direction*)

"Now, loosen your cheeks."
> (*Pinch your cheeks and move them back and forth*)

"Give me a Cheek Wobble."
> (*Growl and shake your cheeks by shaking your head rapidly from side to side*)

"Give me some Teeth Gnashes."
> (*Chomp teeth*)

"And now for the most important storyteller warm-up of all—Tongue Pushups!

Stick out your tongue. . . . Ready! Set! One! Two! One! Two!"
> (*Stick out your tongue and move it up and down*)

"Sideways!"
> (*Move your tongue sideways*)

"Loop-dee-loops!"
> (*Roll your tongue around your mouth in a circle*)

"Other way!"
> (*Reverse direction*)

"Now that everyone is properly warmed up, we can begin our first story!"

Sometimes, older kids will look at me funny when we do the warm-ups. I just tell them that yes, this is goofy, but bear with me. When I talk honestly about what I'm doing with older kids, they usually respond favorably.

## BE EXPRESSIVE

In a typical thirty-minute story program, I usually puff my cheeks, purse my lips, roll my eyes, raise my eyebrows, frown, scowl, wink, blink, lick my lips, jut my chin, wiggle my nose, do double takes, give Jack Benny stares, peer over the top of my glasses, and spit out my water in surprise several times over. Play around and be expressive. Little facial expressions can translate into big laughs. Study the great comedians. Watch videos of Lucille Ball, Red Skelton, Dick Van Dyke, the Marx Brothers, Laurel and Hardy, and other timeless comics. Notice what facial expressions they go through in a short time and how these add to the humor. Look for places in your presentations where you can inject similar expressions. For example, when reading Bill Grossman's *My Little Sister Ate One Hare,* look up from the book and stare at the kids with wide-open eyes and a small rounded mouth whenever the pro-tagonist eats another incredible set of creatures. Or add a variety of shocked looks, looks of disbelief, and looks of resignation. Maintain eye contact with your audience. Notice how they swivel their heads back and forth from the book to your face with big grins of their own.

## FIND YOUR VOICE

When reading or telling a story, remember to enunciate and project. Pace yourself. Don't rush, yet don't read in a slow, monotonous voice. Pacing is more important in drawing out an author's comedic style than simply reading with a silly voice. Don't feel that you need to provide a distinct voice for each character when reading or telling a story. Read the narration in your own voice—with enthusiasm, of course—and select a character or two to highlight with unique, humorous, contrasting voices. It could be two major characters or smaller characters added for comic relief. When I read Keiko Kasza's picture book *The Wolf's Chicken Stew*, I read the chicken's dialogue with an excited, squawking, high-pitched voice. I read the wolf's lines with a low, drawn-out voice, similar to the Walt Disney character Goofy. "Aw, shucks."

Don't make things complicated for yourself or your listeners by providing different voices for a large cast of characters. Bernard Waber's hilarious, tongue-twisting picture book *Bearsie Bear and the Surprise Sleepover Party* has seven animal characters. Give the moose a low voice and the pig a high voice. Read the lines for the other characters and the narrative in your normal or near-normal voice. Too many vocalizations can overkill the comedic effect. The two odd voices will be enough to produce the laughs.

Some authors, like Brian Jacques, author of the Redwall series, are masters at writing dialogue and make the reader's job easier. There's no need to work hard at the vocal distinctions for the various characters. The reader simply goes with the author's flow and direction.

Older listeners, such as middle school-age students, tend to roll their eyes when a reader's character voices are too extreme. They'll laugh when the vocal changes are subtle. When sharing Richard Peck's book *A Long Way from Chicago,* read Grandma Dowdel's lines in a subtle, yet clipped, gruff manner to accentuate the humor of her outrageous character. Don't read them in a stereotypical old woman's voice. With Grandma Dowdel, the laughs come more from her actions than her dialogue.

Add sound effects when appropriate. Exaggerate them once in a while for comedic effect. Instead of making typical animal noises such as "Moo" or "Meow," go for the laughs by going "Mooo-ooo-OOO!" or "Me-ee-ooowwww!" Add an occasional animal sound effect at the end of an animal's dialogue, even if the author hasn't included it in the text. Do the same for vehicle noises, such as tractors, cars, trucks, and rocket ships. Kids love the high-pitched "Beep! Beep! Beep!" sound large vehicles make when they back up.

## EXPERIMENT

One time, on impulse, I pinched my nose to produce a nasal effect while reading the caterpillar's lines in Jack Kent's *The Caterpillar and the Polliwog*:

"When I grow up, I'm going to turn into something else." The caterpillar has a snooty attitude and the nasal sound made it sound snootier. The sight of me holding my nose pointed up in the air gave a visual cue that the caterpillar is a snob. It got a laugh from the audience and encouraged me to keep this little trick in my repertoire.

Another time, I was telling the story of *The Toll-Bridge Troll* by Patricia Rae Wolff. The troll started to sound just like Richard Nixon for no reason at all. It got a laugh from the adults in the audience, so I kept it in the story.

## CREATE YOUR OWN MATERIAL

An easy way to create new material to fit a particular theme is to take a traditional children's song or rhyme and change the lyrics to suit your needs. While I was creating the pig story program included in this book, I spent some time looking at early childhood web sites for inspiration. I found a pig version of "The Wheels on the Bus" that had the following lyrics: "The tail on the pig goes round, round, round. . . . The mouth on the pig goes "oink, oink, oink. . . ." Another site changed the words of "The Ants Go Marching" to "The Pigs Go Marching." Instead of singing the traditional "Hurrah, hurrah," the new version inserts "Oink-oink, oink-oink." I was inspired to create my own pig version of "Old MacDonald Had a Farm" after viewing these sites (see page 24). In the past, I've made new versions of several traditional songs and activities that were well received by children and their parents. These make humorous "story stretchers" to insert between picture books.

Don't limit your sources just because they're labeled for a certain age. Adapt and change good ideas to fit the needs of different age groups. I use a slapstick activity I call "The Super Sticky Bubblegum Game" with all levels of elementary school-age children. The source for this activity is from a recording for two-year-olds. Bob McGrath (Bob from *Sesame Street*) and Katherine Smithrim made a recording titled *Songs and Games for Toddlers* (Kids' Records, 1985). It has an infant activity called "Bubblegum." Basically, kids "stick" their hands together and pull them apart. With the older kids, our "Super Sticky Bubblegum," which we've smeared all over our hands, gets stuck in our hair, on our nose (I start talking in a nasal tone), our cheeks (which in turn make "fish lips"), our eyes ("Are you still there?"), our mouths ("Parents and teachers, would you like me to leave them like this?"), and each other. In between each "sticking" we shout "Unstick! Pull!" This frees our hands until we touch something else. In the end, we throw the bubblegum onto the ceiling, where I say it'll stick until (I then mention a time a few minutes after the program is supposed to end). I never would have found this fun activity if I had stuck to the "appropriate" age-level resources.

## PACE YOURSELF

A nonstop stream of over-the-top laughs is too much. Schedule some peaceful moments between your stories and activities. Add a quiet fingerplay or a gentle song between the funny stuff. This gives you and your audience a break and allows you to build back up to the next humorous piece. With older kids, this gives you a chance to give background information on your stories or have a question-and-answer period.

## AVOID INAPPROPRIATE HUMOR

Most youth services personnel have enough common sense to be aware of the point when good-natured fun becomes mean-spirited. Avoid racist and sexist comments. And never put a child in the spotlight as the object of a joke. Notice the cruel nature of humor on television sitcoms, where the laughs usually come at somebody's expense. Steer away from this type of humor. I do a little gentle teasing of the group as a whole when I make comments like, "Whatever you do, don't laugh," but I'm careful not to make any child feel uncomfortable or embarrassed as a result of my humor.

## FINALLY . . . HAVE FUN

Give yourself permission to be goofy and bigger than life. Smile and dance with abandon. Create a memorable experience for the children and their families. They'll leave knowing that going to the library is fun and that the library may very well be the coolest place in town.

# 2

## Humor Programs for Preschoolers and Primary School-Age Children

I have constructed the following story program lesson plans around four humorous themes: Bad Hair Day, Crazy Critters: Animals That Don't Want to Behave Like Animals, Picky Eaters, and With an Oink-Oink Here and an Oink-Oink There: Piggy Stories. Advertise and post your themes so the audience will know that fun times are ahead. These four models follow a traditional thirty-minute story program format.

### BAD HAIR DAY

#### Program at a Glance

| | |
|---|---|
| PICTURE BOOK | *Franny B. Kranny, There's a Bird in Your Hair!* by Harriet Lerner and Susan Goldhor |
| POEM | "Grandpa's Whiskers" |
| PICTURE BOOK | *Amanda's Perfect Hair* by Linda Milstein |
| MUSICAL ACTIVITY | "Do Your Ears Hang Low?" |
| PICTURE BOOKS | *Big Bushy Mustache* by Gary Soto |
| | *Moosetache* by Margie Palatini |

| POEMS/FELT ACTIVITIES | "There Was an Old Man with a Beard" and "There Was an Old Man in a Tree" by Edward Lear |
| PICTURE BOOK | *Stephanie's Ponytail* by Robert Munsch |
| MUSICAL ACTIVITY | "Michael Finnegan" |

## Preparation and Presentation

Before the presentation, cut out several black construction paper mustaches about six inches in length. Use any simple mustache shape for a pattern, or copy Joe Cepeda's illustrations from the picture book *Big Bushy Mustache* by Gary Soto. Put a loop of tape on the back of each mustache.

Have fun preparing your own hair for the program. Wear a wig or toupee. Use gobs of gel to create spikes, or tease it into a gigantic mess, or color it purple, green, blue—whatever. I have dark brown hair—graying quickly, but never mind. I dyed it platinum blonde one year "for the library." I promised that if the Children's Room signed up a record number of kids for the citywide summer library program, I would color my hair. Of course, my colleagues were outside tackling kids to sign up. You don't have to be that drastic, but be creative and set the tone for Bad Hair Day.

### PICTURE BOOK

Lerner, Harriet, and Susan Goldhor. *Franny B. Kranny, There's a Bird in Your Hair!* Illustrated by Helen Oxenbury. HarperCollins, 2001.

> Franny loves her long, frizzy hair, but it does cause trouble. She gets it caught in her dress buttons and the refrigerator door. To Franny's delight, and her family's horror, a bird lands in her hair and stays.

### POEM

"Grandpa's Whiskers."

> This funny, short, traditional ditty makes a poetry break between the two picture books.

> > Grandpa's whiskers long and gray,
> > Always get in the way.
> > Grandma chews them in her sleep,
> > Thinks that they are shredded wheat.

## PICTURE BOOK

Milstein, Linda. *Amanda's Perfect Hair.* Illustrated by Susan Meddaugh.
Tambourine, 1993.

> This is another story about a girl with wild hair. Amanda is tired of her
> huge, curly, blonde head of hair, so she cuts it before her family can stop
> her. It looks good short, too.

## MUSICAL ACTIVITY

"Do Your Ears Hang Low?"

I've been getting a lot of mileage over the last several years by donning a pair
of tights on my head while singing this song. Even though this particular
story program theme is about hair and not ears, a pair of tights on one's head
can give the appearance of a new hairdo. If you don't know the words to the
song, here they are. If you don't know the tune, ask any group of kids. At
least one of them will know it. It's the tune of "Turkey in the Straw," if that
helps. Move the ends of the tights around and sing:

> Do your ears hang low?
> Do they wobble to and fro?
> Can you tie them in a knot or
> Tie them in a bow?
> Can you throw them over your shoulder
> Like a continental soldier?
> Do your ears hang low?

Since this is a program centered around hair, yank the tights off your
head (provided you were silly enough to put them on in the first place) and
sing the song again with these new "hair" lyrics I adapted:

> Can you wave your hair?
> Can you shake it to and fro?
> Tie it in a knot or
> Tie it in a bow?
> Stick it out the side
> Or did it go and hide?
> Can you wave your hair?

I added the second-to-last line for kids with really short hair (and dads
who have less hair now than when they were kids).

## PICTURE BOOKS

Soto, Gary. *Big Bushy Mustache.* Illustrated by Joe Cepeda. Knopf, 1998.

Little Ricky feels grown up when he wears the fake mustache he received from his teacher. He feels bad when he loses it on the way home. In sympathy, Ricky's father shaves off his own big bushy mustache. "And, hey, now I look just like you!"

Palatini, Margie. *Moosetache.* Illustrated by Henry Cole. Hyperion, 1997.

Moose's overgrown mustache gives him problems. He makes a moose-scarf out of it, but it chokes him. He makes "moosetachioed antlers" until squirrels move in. He tries a moose-tail (a moose-type ponytail), but that doesn't work either. He finally meets the moose of his dreams, who comes up with the perfect solution.

At the end of the last two picture books, let the children line up and place the construction paper mustaches on any stuffed animals or puppets you have. The kids won't mind if you don't have a moose, as long as they can stick the mustaches on any animal. This brief activity is a nice tie-in to the books and a chance to move around a little.

## POEMS/FELT ACTIVITIES

"There Was an Old Man with a Beard" and "There Was an Old Man in a
Tree" by Edward Lear.

Both poems can be found in many Lear anthologies. Cut out a large beard-shaped piece of felt for "There Was an Old Man with a Beard." Cut several separate long strands out of the beard. Place them together on the felt board to look like the original whole beard. Make simple felt circles to represent the two owls, hen, four larks, and wren that make nests in the old man's beard. Place the circles on the beard as you recite the lines. Next, start reciting "There Was an Old Man in a Tree." This poem describes birds plucking his beard to make their nests. Pull the various strands of the beard and make them disappear.

## PICTURE BOOK

Munsch, Robert. *Stephanie's Ponytail.* Illustrated by Michael Martchenko.
Annick, 1996.

Stephanie goes to school wearing her ponytail in different styles each day. The other children mock her and then show up the next day imitating her hairstyle. In the end, Stephanie warns them that she's going to shave her head completely bald. Everyone shows up the next day completely bald. All except Stephanie. There are many fun ways to present this story. Long-haired storytellers can move their ponytails around on their own head while telling the story. Short-haired storytellers can wear a long wig. Or you can use a long-haired doll as a story prop. The text also makes a great reader's theater presentation. Write parts for Stephanie, her mother, and four narrators who not only split up the narration, but also recite the school kids' lines.

## MUSICAL ACTIVITY

"Michael Finnegan."

Teach the children the words to this simple traditional song.

> There once was a man named Michael Finnegan.
> He grew whiskers on his chin-igin.
> Shaved them off, but they grew in-igin.
> Poor old Michael Finnegan.
> Begin again.

Sing or chant the song over and over. Vary the tempo, pitch, and volume each time for fun. ("Sing it really slow. Now, sing it in a whisper.") You may also want to share Mary Ann Hoberman's picture book *There Once Was a Man Named Michael Finnegan,* illustrated by Nadine Bernard Westcott (Little, Brown, 2001).

As the children leave the room, attach a construction paper mustache to their upper lip with transparent tape (don't force anybody to wear one). The sight of children wandering around the library in fake mustaches will, no doubt, leave parents, bystanders, and staff in stitches.

## ADDITIONAL HUMOROUS HAIR PICTURE BOOKS

Hunt, Angela Elwell. *If I Had Long, Long Hair.* Illustrated by L. Diane Johnson. Abingdon, 1988.

> Young Loretta Littlefield wishes for long, long hair. She imagines using her braids as jump ropes, streaming behind her in a parade, and sweeping the kitchen floor as she walks across it. Then Loretta starts imagining the bad things that could happen to a girl with long, long hair.

Munsch, Robert. *Aaron's Hair.* Illustrated by Alan and Lea Daniel. Scholastic, 2000.

> Aaron's hair runs right off the top of his head and attaches itself to a lady's tummy, a man's behind, a policeman's face, a statue's head, and then back onto Aaron—as a beard on his chin.

Palatini, Margie. *Mooseltoe.* Illustrated by Henry Cole. Hyperion, 2000.

> Moose is back and so is his extremely large "moosetache." He is all set for Christmas ("Check. Check. Check"), but then realizes he forgot a Christmas tree. All the trees around town are sold out. With the help of some glue, he and his family fashion a tree out of his mustache and hang lights and decorations on it.

# CRAZY CRITTERS: ANIMALS THAT DON'T WANT TO BEHAVE LIKE ANIMALS

## Program at a Glance

| | |
|---|---|
| PICTURE BOOKS | *Parents in the Pigpen, Pigs in the Tub* by Amy Ehrlich |
| | *Milo's Hat Trick* by Jon Agee |
| | *Animals Should Definitely Not Wear Clothing* by Judi Barrett |
| MUSICAL ACTIVITY | "I Had a Rooster" |
| PICTURE BOOKS | *Widget* by Lyn Rossiter McFarland |
| | *Bark, George* by Jules Feiffer |
| MUSICAL ACTIVITY | "The Animals in the Zoo" adapted by Rob Reid |
| PICTURE BOOK | *Click, Clack, Moo: Cows That Type* by Doreen Cronin |

## Preparation and Presentation

Ask the children what they think might happen if animals started acting like people or other animals. Ask them what they would think if their pets started sitting at the dining table with them or going to the movies.

## PICTURE BOOKS

Ehrlich, Amy. *Parents in the Pigpen, Pigs in the Tub*. Illustrated by Steven Kellogg. Dial, 1993.

> The animals decide they'd rather live in the farmer's house than in the barn. To add to the absurdity, Mom initially says that it's all right with her. Soon, the chickens demand cornflakes instead of shredded wheat, the pigs demand a fair share of the bathroom, the horses hog the television, and the humans find themselves out in the barn.

Agee, Jon. *Milo's Hat Trick*. Hyperion, 2001.

> Milo the Magnificent was not a magnificent magician at all. While fishing for a rabbit to pull out of his hat, Milo catches a bear who teaches him the trick of jumping into a hat. "You just pretend your bones are made of rubber." The illustration of the bear popping out of the hat in a restaurant and going "TA-DA!" is precious.

Barrett, Judi. *Animals Should Definitely Not Wear Clothing*. Illustrated by Ron Barrett. Atheneum, 1970.

> Read this very short picture book with wide-eyed astonishment as you come across visual humor such as a giraffe wearing several neckties, a hen with the outline of an egg in the rear of her pants, and an elephant wearing the same dress pattern and hat as a woman who is visiting the zoo. Companion book: *Animals Should Definitely Not Act like People*. Atheneum, 1980.

## MUSICAL ACTIVITY

Lithgow, John. "I Had a Rooster." On *Singin' in the Bathtub* (Recording). Sony, 1999.

Listen to Lithgow's wild version of this traditional folk song. His animal noises are over the top. Use his style to model this activity for your audience. Teach everyone the chorus:

> I had a rooster and the rooster pleased me.
> I fed my rooster 'neath the old chestnut tree.
> My little rooster went cock-a-doodle-doo, dee-doodle, dee-doodle,
> dee-doodle, dee-doo.

Next ask the kids for animal suggestions. No matter what type of animal they suggest, make wildly exaggerated noises for that animal, à la Lithgow. Instead of singing "Woof" for a dog, sing "Woo-woo-woof-woof-ah-whoo-ooo-ooo!" Instead of singing "Meow" for a cat, sing "Hsst, spit, rarrrr-eee-owww." Have the children imitate you. If a child suggests an animal that's hard to use with a noise, invent dialogue for the animal. A giraffe, for example, might say, "Hey! Look way up here!" Add other animals to the mix, like monkeys, lions, whales, and elephants. Everyone should stand and act out a motion for each animal as it bellows.

## PICTURE BOOKS

McFarland, Lyn Rossiter. *Widget*. Illustrated by Jim McFarland. Farrar, 2001.

> Mrs. Diggs's cats, "the girls," don't like the new stray dog. However, he wins them over by meowing, puffing, hissing, spitting, and growling. When Mrs. Diggs passes out, and the cats' growls don't attract anyone, Widget, the dog, begins to bark. The cats join in with their own barks, and help soon arrives. Great illustrations of "the girls" and Widget having a puffing standoff.

Feiffer, Jules. *Bark, George*. HarperCollins, 1999.

> George, a puppy, meows, quacks, oinks, and moos, much to his mother's dismay. Begin reading her lines with parental patience before giving way to frustration. When the vet begins pulling animals out of George's throat, react incredulously.

## MUSICAL ACTIVITY

"The Animals in the Zoo" adapted by Rob Reid.

There are several variations of using animal noises to the tune of "The Wheels on the Bus." Here's a version that, while set at the zoo, can use animals from all habitats. Use your imagination. Ask the audience to come up with other funny noises and activities that animals found in the zoo (virtually any animal or bird) can make in an exaggerated manner.

> The monkeys in the zoo go Ooh-ooh-ohh, Ooh-ooh-ohh, Ooh-ooh-ohh,
> The monkeys in the zoo go Ooh-ooh-ooh all the day and night.

The hippos in the zoo go Yawn-yawn-yawn, Yawn-yawn-yawn, Yawn-yawn-yawn,
The hippos in the zoo go Yawn-yawn-yawn all the day and night.
The beavers in the zoo go Timmmmberrrr! Timmmmberrrr! Timmmmberrrr!
The beavers in the zoo go Timmmmberrrr! all the day and night.

## PICTURE BOOK

Cronin, Doreen. *Click, Clack, Moo: Cows That Type*. Illustrated by Betsy Lewin. Simon & Schuster, 2000.

This Caldecott Honor Book has humor on several levels. The younger children will laugh at the antics of the farm animals. The older listeners will enjoy the tactics of a labor struggle. Let the kids play with a real typewriter to end both the story and the story program. Let each child type for a few seconds. The line should move along at a fast clip. As one local library reported, "Some of the kids can type 982 letters a minute."

## ADDITIONAL HUMOROUS PICTURE BOOKS
## ABOUT CRAZY CRITTERS

Himmelman, John. *A Guest Is a Guest*. Dutton, 1991.

Farmer Beanbuckets and his family are overrun by the farm animals who take over the house. The farmer takes it all in stride. "A guest is a guest, and we must show them our best," he says. Eventually, their patience runs out, but before they can remove the animals, the animals toss the Beanbuckets out.

Johnson, Paul Brett. *The Cow Who Wouldn't Come Down*. Orchard, 1993.

Miss Rosemary is in a tizzy because Gertrude, her cow, starts flying over the homestead. Enjoy reading the unique sentences: "Miss Rosemary hadn't the slightest clue how to milk a flying cow" or "That crackbrained cow will put me in an early grave."

Rathmann, Peggy. *Good Night, Gorilla*. Putnam, 1994.

A small gorilla snitches the zookeeper's keys and frees the other animals. Instead of fleeing, they follow the unsuspecting zookeeper into his house and settle down for the evening. They aren't discovered until they all say "Good night." The book contains few words, but lots of laughs.

Yee, Wong Herbert. *Mrs. Brown Went to Town.* Houghton Mifflin, 1996.

Mrs. Brown lived with "a cow, two pigs, three ducks, and a yak." When she becomes injured and is sent to the hospital, the animals move into her house. They eat her food, wear her gowns, put on her makeup, bounce on her bed, paint her house red, and flush the toilet "one hundred times."

# PICKY EATERS

## Program at a Glance

| | |
|---|---|
| ACTIVITY | "The World's Worst Ice-Cream Store" by Rob Reid |
| PICTURE BOOKS | *Eat Your Peas* by Kes Gray |
| | *My Little Sister Ate One Hare* by Bill Grossman |
| MUSICAL ACTIVITY | "I Know an Old Lady Who Swallowed a Dinosaur" by Rob Reid |
| PICTURE BOOK | *I Know an Old Lady Who Swallowed a Pie* by Alison Jackson |
| MUSICAL ACTIVITY | "Jelly, Jelly in My Belly" |
| PICTURE BOOKS | *I Will Never Not Ever Eat a Tomato* by Lauren Child |
| | *Here Comes Henny* by Charlotte Pomerantz |
| MOVEMENT ACTIVITY | "Don't Eat That!" by Rob Reid |

## Preparation and Presentation

**ACTIVITY**

"The World's Worst Ice-Cream Store" by Rob Reid.

Cut out several rectangular pieces of poster board or construction paper approximately 10″ x 4″. These will be used to announce the flavors of the day for "The World's Worst Ice-Cream Store." Ask the children to name their favorite ice-cream flavors. After they finish going through the usual flavors, tell them that you know an ice-cream store that serves terrible flavors. Make up examples such as Liver and Onions Ice Cream, Lima Bean Sherbet, and Dogfood Delight. Write these flavors on your rectangles and stick them to the wall. Then ask the children to suggest other terrible flavors, and post those on the wall, too. You have created "The World's Worst Ice-Cream Store" and set the tone for the Picky Eaters story program.

## PICTURE BOOKS

Gray, Kes. *Eat Your Peas.* Illustrated by Nick Sharratt. Dorling Kindersley, 2000.

> Mom's bribes to get Daisy to eat her peas quickly escalate from "If you eat your peas, you can have a dish of ice cream" to Mom promising everything in the universe "and . . . and . . . and . . . and a new fluffy pencil cap." Read Mom's dialogue with increasing desperation, while Daisy grows more and more stubborn.

Grossman, Bill. *My Little Sister Ate One Hare.* Illustrated by Kevin Hawkes. Crown, 1996.

> Little sister has no problem eating one hare, two snakes, three ants, four shrews, five bats, six mice "she spit out and ate twice," seven polliwogs, eight worms, and nine lizards. She does, however, have a problem with ten peas. (What is it with peas?) Kids will contribute to the experience with frequent "Ee-uu-ww's."

## MUSICAL ACTIVITY

"I Know an Old Lady Who Swallowed a Dinosaur" by Rob Reid.

Read the opening poem and then sing or chant the extra verses while holding up pictures of a yak, moose, polar bear, shark, dinosaur, and whale.

> I know an old lady who swallowed a dinosaur.
> Swallowed a dinosaur? Oh, please tell me more!
> It all began when she swallowed a fly.
> She started to cry, "I'm gonna die!"
> She swallowed a spider to catch the fly.
> Why she did that, well, I don't know why.
> She swallowed a bird, a cat, dog and goat.
> All of those critters went—Gulp!—down her throat.
> She swallowed a cow. She swallowed a horse.
> Most folks 'round here thought that she'd had her last course.
> But all of those creatures were still in her tummy.

She had to find something much bigger—and yummy.
So—
I know an old lady who swallowed a yak.
It made a nice snack, that yakkity yak.
She swallowed the yak to catch all the rest
From the galloping horse to that buzzing fly pest.
She swallowed the fly. I cannot lie.
I don't know why she swallowed a fly.
Perhaps she'll die.

I know an old lady who swallowed a moose.
It almost got loose, but she munched down that moose.
She swallowed the moose to catch the yak.
She swallowed the yak to catch all the rest
From the galloping horse to the buzzing fly pest.
She swallowed that fly. I cannot lie.
I don't know why she swallowed a fly.
Perhaps she'll die.

I know an old lady who swallowed a polar bear.
It didn't have a prayer, that poor polar bear.
She swallowed the bear to catch the moose.
She swallowed the moose to catch the yak.
She swallowed the yak to catch all the rest
From the galloping horse to the buzzing fly pest.
She swallowed that fly. I cannot lie.
I don't know why she swallowed a fly.
Perhaps she'll die.

I know an old lady who swallowed a shark.
Oh, what a lark to snarf down a shark.
She swallowed the shark to catch the bear.
She swallowed the bear to catch the moose.
She swallowed the moose to catch the yak.
She swallowed the yak to catch all the rest
From the galloping horse to the buzzing fly pest.
She swallowed that fly. I cannot lie.
I don't know why she swallowed a fly.
Perhaps she'll die.

I know an old lady who swallowed a dinosaur.
Oh, she was very, very sore.
She swallowed a dinosaur to catch a shark.
She swallowed a shark to catch a bear.
She swallowed a bear to catch a moose.
She swallowed a moose to catch a yak.
She swallowed a yak to catch all the rest
From the galloping horse to the buzzing fly pest.
She swallowed that fly. I cannot lie.
I don't know why she swallowed a fly.
Perhaps she'll die.

I know an old lady who swallowed a whale.
That's the end of this tale.

## PICTURE BOOK

Jackson, Alison. *I Know an Old Lady Who Swallowed a Pie.* Illustrated by Judith Byron Schachner. Dutton, 1997.

An old lady comes over for a Thanksgiving dinner, eats the entire meal, and winds up as a holiday parade float.

## MUSICAL ACTIVITY

"Jelly, Jelly in My Belly."

The words to the original song can be found in my book *Family Storytime* (ALA, 1999). Ask the children to think of their least-favorite food to include in this picky eater version. This traditional song can be chanted.

2-4-6-8, tell me what is on your plate!
We're going to have some spinach! Hurray! Hurray!
We're going to have some spinach! Hurray! Hurray!
Spinach for our dinner. Spinach every day.
Spinach, spinach, in our belly.
Hip, hip, hip, hooray!

2-4-6-8, tell me what is on your plate!
We're going to have anchovies. Hurray! Hurray!
We're going to have anchovies. Hurray! Hurray!
Anchovies for our dinner. Anchovies every day.

And spinach, spinach, in our belly.
Hip, hip, hip, hooray!

2-4-6-8, tell me what is on your plate!

Add suggestions from the audience and tag them onto the end of the chant. If children suggest a type of food that most people enjoy, go ahead and add it in. You might end up with a nice mix of healthy, enjoyable food for some and not-so-pleasant foods for others.

## PICTURE BOOKS

Child, Lauren. *I Will Never Not Ever Eat a Tomato*. Candlewick, 2000.

Charlie tricks Lola into eating healthier by giving each food item a new identity. Thus, carrots become orange twiglets from Jupiter, peas are green drops from Greenland, mashed potatoes are cloud fluffs from Mount Fuji, fish sticks are ocean nibbles, and the dreaded tomatoes are moonsquirters. Ask the children to come up with new names for common foods. One group recently called hamburgers miniature manhole covers from the moon, and bananas were dubbed golden giant eyebrows from Kansas.

Pomerantz, Charlotte. *Here Comes Henny*. Illustrated by Nancy Winslow Parker. Greenwillow, 1994.

This tongue-twisting, rebus story shows Henny bringing healthy food for her picky chicks. "Pick pick pick a snicky." But they reply, "We eat only snacky-snicky." The kids will giggle at the alliteration. The book ends with a loud "Cluck!" as Henny catches the chicks overflowing their backpack with snacks for their "picnic-nicky."

## MOVEMENT ACTIVITY

"Don't Eat That" by Rob Reid.

While saying the lines, the leader can either have one child do the corresponding activity or ask the whole group to do them.

1. Hey you! Don't eat that pie!
   Don'tcha know it'll make you cry?
   (*Make big crying noises*)
2. Hey you! Don't eat that cheese!
   Don'tcha know it'll make you sneeze?
   (*Give a big ah-choo*)

3. Beans . . . mean.
   (*Make an angry face*)

4. Cake . . . shake.
   (*Shake whole body*)

5. Veal . . . squeal.
   (*Squeal like a pig*)

6. Trout . . . pout.
   (*Stick out lower lip*)

7. Grape . . . act like an ape.
   (*Make ape noises and gestures*)

8. Honey . . . funny.
   (*Laugh hysterically*)

9. Onion rings . . . sing.
   (*Sing la-la-la*)

10. Peach . . . reach.
    (*Reach to the sky*)

11. Fruit . . . look real cute.
    (*Finger on chin and flutter eyes*)

12. Chili . . . look real silly.
    (*Finger on chin and flutter eyes again*)

13. Ice cream . . . scream.
    (*Scream and then ask, "Didn't you always want to do that in a library?"*)

14. Bun . . . now we're all done.
    (*Clap hands*)

Sometimes I'll end by saying, "No, don't eat any of that! Give it all to *me!*" After the program, serve delicious orange twiglets from Jupiter and golden giant eyebrows from Kansas.

## ADDITIONAL HUMOROUS BOOKS
## ABOUT PICKY EATERS

Demarest, Chris. *No Peas for Nellie.* Macmillan, 1988.

Nellie would rather eat a big, furry spider; a wet, slimy salamander; a hairy warthog; a pair of aardvarks; a python; a big, old crocodile; a water buffalo; a lion; a giraffe; and an elephant rather than her pile of peas.

(Peas again!) The audience will once more, no doubt, contribute a significant number of "Yucks" and "Ee-uu-ww's" throughout your reading.

Hoberman, Mary Ann. *The Seven Silly Eaters.* Illustrated by Marla Frazee. Harcourt, 1997.

Mrs. Peters's seven children are very picky eaters, but she sets out to please each one. When son Mac finds a lump in his oatmeal, he dumps it on the cat. As her children and their appetites grow, so does the chaos.

Napoli, Donna Jo, and Richard Tchen. *How Hungry Are You?* Illustrated by Amy Walrod. Atheneum, 2001.

Two animals are headed to a picnic. One by one, others join in. They wind up trying to determine how to divide the food. There are several funny bits, such as the frog looking for any type of watermelon-flavored food. The unusual format of all dialogue (no narration) and character lines marked by symbols make this a good reader's theater choice.

Yaccarino, Dan. *The Lima Bean Monster.* Illustrated by Adam McCauley. Walker, 2001.

Sammy buries his plate of lima beans in a vacant lot. Other kids catch on and bury their unwanted vegetables in the same location. When lightning strikes the ground, a Lima Bean Monster comes to life. Wave a piece of poster board throughout the story for a humorous thunder sound effect.

# WITH AN OINK-OINK HERE AND AN OINK-OINK THERE: PIGGY STORIES

## Program at a Glance

| | |
|---|---|
| PICTURE BOOK | *Piggie Pig* by Margie Palatini |
| MUSICAL ACTIVITY | "Old MacDonald Had a Pig" adapted by Rob Reid |
| PICTURE BOOK | *Olivia* by Ian Falconer |
| MUSICAL ACTIVITY | "P-O-R-K-Y" adapted by Rob Reid |
| PICTURE BOOK | *If You Give a Pig a Pancake* by Laura Joffe Numeroff |

| | |
|---|---|
| POEM | "There Was a Small Pig Who Wept Tears," in *The Book of Pigericks* by Arnold Lobel |
| FINGERPLAY | "This Little Piggy" |
| PICTURE BOOK | *Five Little Piggies* by David Martin |
| POEM | "Little Pig's Treat," in *Falling Up* by Shel Silverstein. |
| MUSICAL ACTIVITY | "I'm a Little Piggy" |
| PICTURE BOOK | *Z-Z-Zoink!* by Bernard Most |
| MUSICAL ACTIVITIES | "The Higgy-Piggy" |
| | "Hippo Hop Hokey Pokey" by Kati Tvruska |

## Preparation and Presentation

Cut out several pink circles. Mark them with two black ovals or "nostrils." Put a loop of transparent tape on the back of each circle. Wear one on your nose and ask the children as they enter if they want a piggie nose. Don't force them to wear one. Allow them to get a piggie nose later on during the program.

## PICTURE BOOK

Palatini, Margie. *Piggie Pie.* Illustrated by Howard Fine. Clarion, 1995.

> Gritch the witch needs eight plump piggies for piggie pie. She heads over the river and through the woods to Old MacDonald's Farm (she sees his ad in the yellow pages instructing her to call EI-EI-O). The pigs disguise themselves as ducks, cows, chickens, and Old MacDonald himself. This is a long story, but lively enough to keep the audience's attention. The illustrations have sly references that will appeal to adults (the witch flying overhead spelling out "Surrender Piggies" in the style of *The Wizard of Oz* movie). You may want to keep the Wicked Witch of the West in mind as you read Gritch's lines aloud. The story has countless references to the song "Old MacDonald Had a Farm." Since the pigs are disguised as other animals, they "quack-quack here" and "moo-moo there" and "cluck-cluck everywhere."

**MUSICAL ACTIVITY**

"Old MacDonald Had a Pig" adapted by Rob Reid.

Tell the children that some people think pigs go "oink-oink" while others think pigs grunt, squeal, or snort. Sing "Old MacDonald Had a Farm" using various pig sounds.

1. Old MacDonald had a farm. EI-EI-O.
   And on his farm he had a pig. EI-EI-O.
   With an oink-oink here and an oink-oink there.
   Here an oink. There an oink. Everywhere an oink-oink.
   Old MacDonald had a farm. EI-EI-O.

2. . . . with a grunt-grunt here and a grunt-grunt there . . .

3. . . . with a squeal-squeal here and a squeal-squeal there . . .

4. . . . with a snort-snort here and a snort-snort there . . .

**PICTURE BOOK**

Falconer, Ian. *Olivia*. Atheneum, 2000.

Olivia the pig is very good at wearing people out. She tries on several outfits, builds sand skyscrapers on the beach, dreams of becoming a ballerina after looking at a Degas painting, and paints an abstract work of art on her bedroom wall after viewing a Jackson Pollock. Read the book in your normal voice and give the children time to pore over the unique drawings. They'll giggle at Olivia's sunburned body. The best line in the book occurs when Olivia's mother tells her that despite wearing her out, she loves her anyway. Olivia kisses her and says, "I love you anyway too." Sequel: *Olivia Saves the Circus* (Atheneum, 2001).

**MUSICAL ACTIVITY**

"P-O-R-K-Y" adapted by Rob Reid.

I often adapt the traditional song "B-I-N-G-O" into new versions that fit the theme for that day: "D-A-I-S-Y" for a cow theme, "K-I-T-T-Y" for cats, "S-Q-E-A-K" for mice, and so on. Make an "oink" noise instead of a clap when you drop each letter.

There was a farmer had a pig and Porky was his name-O.
P-O-R-K-Y, P-O-R-K-Y, P-O-R-K-Y
And Porky was his name-O.

There was a farmer had a pig and Porky was his name-O.
(Oink)-O-R-K-Y, (Oink)-O-R-K-Y, (Oink)-O-R-K-Y
And Porky was his name-O.
There was a farmer had a pig and Porky was his name-O.
(Oink)-(Oink)-R-K-Y, (Oink)-(Oink)-R-K-Y, (Oink)-(Oink)-R-K-Y
And Porky was his name-O.

And so on until the final verse:

There was a farmer had a pig and Porky was his name-O.
Oink-Oink-Oink-Oink-Oink,
Oink-Oink-Oink-Oink-Oink,
Oink-Oink-Oink-Oink-Oink,
And Porky was his name-O.

## PICTURE BOOK

Numeroff, Laura Joffe. *If You Give a Pig a Pancake.* Illustrated by Felicia
Bond. HarperCollins, 1998.

This nonsensical book follows the same pattern of Numeroff's and Bond's
successful If You Give a Mouse a Cookie series. The kids will giggle at
the antics of the pig and the little girl who star in the book.

## POEM

Lobel, Arnold. "There Was a Small Pig Who Wept Tears." In *The Book of
Pigericks.* HarperCollins, 1983.

Mention that pigs like to lie in the mud. This poem details the anguish
of a little pig who takes a bath hoping "This won't happen again for ten
years!" Other favorite individual "pigericks" include "There Was a Sad
Pig with a Tail," "There Was a Warm Pig from Key West," and "There
Was a Small Pig from Woonsocket."

## FINGERPLAY

"This Little Piggy."

Use the traditional nursery rhyme to give the kids a chance to move a little
and to introduce the next picture book. Tell them to point to their toes
"beneath your shoes," but if some insist on taking off their shoes and socks,
go with the flow.

This little piggy went to the market.
> (*Wiggle big toe*)

This little piggy stayed home.
> (*Wiggle second toe*)

This little piggy had roast beef.
> (*Wiggle third toe*)

This little piggy had none.
> (*Wiggle fourth toe*)

And this little piggy said "Wee-wee-wee" all the way home.
> (*Wiggle little toe*)

## PICTURE BOOK

Martin, David. *Five Little Piggies*. Illustrated by Susan Meddaugh. Candlewick, 1998.

> Martin creates mini-stories for each of the piggies mentioned in the nursery rhyme. The highlight comes at the end of the book, when the littlest piggie cries "Wee-wee-wee" all the way home because she has to go "wee-wee."

## POEM

Silverstein, Shel. "Little Pig's Treat." In *Falling Up*. HarperCollins, 1996.

> Little pig wants pop pig to give him a "people-back ride."

## MUSICAL ACTIVITY

"I'm a Little Piggy" (to the tune of "I'm a Little Teapot").

I found this version on several early childhood web sites.

I'm a little piggy
> (*Point to self*)

Short and stout.

Here are my ears
> (*Point to ears*)

Here is my snout.
> (*Point to nose*)

When I see the

Farmer in the dell
   (*Hand over eyes*)
I oink, oink, oink
and wiggle my tail.
   (*Shake hips*)

## PICTURE BOOK

Most, Bernard. *Z-Z-Zoink!* Harcourt, 1999.

A pig snores loud enough to wake all the barnyard animals plus the farmer and his family. There are a lot of opportunities for the audience to make sound effects as the cows "moo" the pig away and the sheep "baa" her away. The ducks, chickens, goats, and frogs all join the noisy fun. Have the audience make "shoo" hand gestures during the appropriate times. The pig finally finds comfort in the company of owls. Good luck getting the children to stop "hooting."

## MUSICAL ACTIVITIES

"The Higgy-Piggy" (to the tune of "The Hokey Pokey").

This number can also be found on several early childhood web sites.

You put your right hoof in,
You put your right hoof out,
You put your right hoof in and you shake it all about.
You do the Higgy-Piggy and you turn yourself around.
That's what it's all about. Oink!
   (*Repeat with verses for left hoof, hamhock, snout, tail*)

"Hippo Hop Hokey Pokey" by Kati Tvruska.

For an extra treat, you can do a hippopotamus version of "The Hokey Pokey." Tell the children that hippos remind you of very large pigs.

You put your clean foot in,
You take your dirty foot out.
You put your clean foot in,
And you squash it all about.
You do the Hippo Hop and you hop down in the mud.

That's what a hippo does!
*(Repeat with verses for snout, legs, tail)*

## ADDITIONAL HUMOROUS PIG PICTURE BOOKS

Alarcon, Karen Beaumont. *Louella Mae, She's Run Away!* Illustrated by
  Rosanne Litzinger. Holt, 1997.

> Everyone is searching for Louella Mae. The layout is designed for the
> audience to shout out the last rhyme of each stanza. In the end, Louella
> Mae turns out to be a pig with new piglets asleep in a tub.

Enderle, Judith Ross, and Stephanie Gordon Tessler. *A Pile of Pigs.*
  Illustrated by Charles Jordan. Bell Books, 1993.

> The pigs make a Super Duper Pig Pyramid to see what the cows are doing
> on the other side of the barn. Make several simple pig-shaped felt pieces,
> even if they are nothing more than circles with pig faces on them. Pile
> them in a pyramid shape as the story progresses. Have the audience sway
> as the pig pyramid sways back and forth. And what were the cows doing
> on the other side of the barn? They were building a pyramid to see what
> the pigs were doing.

Meddaugh, Susan. *Hog-Eye.* Houghton Mifflin, 1995.

> A little pig tells some mighty tall tales about walking in the forest alone
> and encountering a wolf who has plans to make pig soup. The pig
> escapes by outwitting the illiterate wolf. She tells him the recipe needs
> "green three leaf," which turns out to be poison ivy. She pretends to cast
> a spell on him, making him itchy everywhere—"On his nose and in his
> hair/Even in his underwear." The pig's family makes funny comments
> throughout the little pig's story.

# 3

## Humor Programs for Intermediate School-Age Children

Librarians need to develop different strategies when dealing with humor programs for children who are beyond the preschool and primary ages. This section will demonstrate how to create story programs for older students using the traditional story program format, special events, and theme parties.

### TRADITIONAL STORY PROGRAM FORMAT

Intermediate school-age children will attend library story programs if they are called anything but "story programs." The term has too many connotations to preschool story programs. If you run a series of story programs for intermediate school-age children, give it a snappy name, such as The Crazy Club or Razzle-Dazzle Drop-In. Advertise heavily at the elementary schools. Mention in your fliers that younger children will not be allowed to attend. They will scare away the target audience—I speak from experience.

When planning this type of library program, follow a format similar to the traditional preschool story program. Add more oral storytelling or read-aloud selections from chapter books. It's okay to sneak in a few picture books once in a while. Many picture books today are being written for this age group. Make sure your program theme appeals to this age group. The model program School Daze takes advantage of the many excellent resources that feature school, students, and teachers.

# SCHOOL DAZE

## Lesson Plan at a Glance

| | |
|---|---|
| POEM | "Sick" by Shel Silverstein, in *Where the Sidewalk Ends* |
| ORAL STORY | *The Toll-Bridge Troll* by Patricia Rae Wolff |
| SONG | "I Don't Want to Go to School" by Barry Louis Polisar from the recording *Teacher's Favorites* |
| POEM | "Mrs. Stein" by Bill Dodds, in *Kids Pick the Funniest Poems,* edited by Bruce Lansky |
| PICTURE BOOK | *School Picture Day* by Lynne Plourde |
| READ-ALOUD | Selection from *Junie B. Jones Has a Monster Under Her Bed* by Barbara Park |
| PICTURE BOOK | *Moira's Birthday* by Robert Munsch |
| POEM | "Homework! Oh, Homework!" by Jack Prelutsky, in *The New Kid on the Block* |
| ORAL STORY | "Sarah's Story" by Bill Harley from the recording *Come on Out and Play* |

## Preparation and Presentation

**POEM**

Silverstein, Shel. "Sick." In *Where the Sidewalk Ends.* HarperCollins, 1974.

Little Peggy Ann McKay recites a litany of ailments from "purple bumps" to "a hole inside my ear." Then she learns that "today is . . . Saturday?"

Memorize this poem and act it out on a table with a blanket. Start out prone and quiet. Slowly get up as you recite the lines louder and louder. By the time you reach the punch line, you should be standing.

**ORAL STORY**

Wolff, Patricia Rae. *The Toll-Bridge Troll.* Illustrated by Kimberly Bulcken Root. Harcourt, 1995.

A young boy, headed for school, outwits a troll by asking a series of riddles. When the troll is tricked for the third time, he winds up going to school with the boy.

This is one of my all-time favorite stories to tell, and it's more fun without the book because I'm free to use my whole body when explaining the riddles. Keep a penny and a nickel in your pocket for the third riddle.

## SONG

Polisar, Barry. "I Don't Want to Go to School." On *Teacher's Favorites* (Recording). Rainbow Morning Music, 1993.

Tommy tells his mother that he doesn't want to go to school because "no one likes me there" and "the children there are not nice." The punch line reveals that Tommy is the school's principal. This recording has other humorous school songs, such as "I've Got a Teacher, She's So Mean." The recording can be purchased on Polisar's web site: www. barrylou.com.

## POEM

Dodds, Bill. "Mrs. Stein." In *Kids Pick the Funniest Poems,* edited by Bruce Lansky. Meadowbrook, 1991.

This long story poem describes a six-foot-eight substitute teacher who knocks the door off its hinges and makes the school bully wet his pants. By the end of the day, the children are praying for the health of their regular classroom teacher.

## PICTURE BOOK

Plourde, Lynne. *School Picture Day.* Illustrated by Thor Wickstrom. Dutton, 2002.

All of the students are excited about picture day except Josephina Caroleena Wattasheena the First. She's more interested in repairing a gear shaft, the pencil sharpener, and the sprinkler and heating systems. Her messing about gets everyone filthy for their pictures. The day is saved when Josephina fixes the photographer's broken camera. Delight in the language: "Everyone, say cheesy wheezy, if you pleasy."

## READ-ALOUD

Park, Barbara. *Junie B. Jones Has a Monster Under Her Bed.* Random, 1997.

The first chapter of this volume is my favorite of all the Junie B. Jones series. The school photographer gets "fusstation" in him when Junie B.

doesn't cooperate. He winds up taking her picture while she's making a funny face. Her friend Lucille comments that "the camera is my friend," and Paulie Allen Puffer tries to convince Junie B. that the drool on her pillow is from the monster that lives under her bed.

## PICTURE BOOK

Munsch, Robert. *Moira's Birthday*. Illustrated by Michael Martchenko. Annick, 1987.

Moira invites the whole school to her birthday party. The audience will chime in when she says, ". . . aaaaaaand kindergarten."

## POEM

Prelutsky, Jack. "Homework! Oh, Homework!" In *The New Kid on the Block*. Greenwillow, 1984.

The narrator would rather take baths with sharks, pet porcupines, and eat liver and spinach than do homework. This poem can also be found in the book *I Thought I'd Take My Rat to School: Poems for September to June*, edited by Dorothy M. Kennedy (Little, Brown, 1993).

## ORAL STORY

Harley, Bill. "Sarah's Story." On *Come on Out and Play* (Recording). Round River, 1990.

Sarah is upset about her storytelling homework. On the way to school, she enters an ant colony and a beehive. This is a fun, animated story to tell. Even though a picture book version is available (Tricycle Press, 1996), the kids will get more out of the story if you memorize it. Harley has other school-related storytelling and music recordings available on his web site: www.billharley.com. Titles include: *Cool in School* (Round River, 1987); *From the Back of the Bus* (Round River, 1995); *Lunchroom Tales: A Natural History of the Cafetorium* (Round River, 1996).

## ADDITIONAL HUMOROUS BOOKS ABOUT SCHOOL

Marshall, James. *The Cut-Ups Cut Loose*. Viking, 1987.

Troublemakers Spud and Joe head off to school with their supplies of spitballs, stink bombs, and Joe's pet tarantula. They run into their new principal, Lamar J. Spurgle. Companion books: *The Cut-Ups* (Viking, 1984); *The Cut-Ups at Camp Custer* (Viking, 1989); *The Cut-Ups Carry On* (Viking, 1990); *The Cut-Ups Crack Up* (Viking, 1992).

Munsch, Robert. *Thomas' Snowsuit*. Illustrated by Michael Martchenko. Annick, 1985.

Thomas refuses to wear his new brown snowsuit. His teacher tells him to put it on, but Thomas says, "NNNNNO." After a struggle, his teacher winds up wearing the snowsuit and her dress ends up on Thomas. Then the principal arrives. . . .

Pulver, Robin. *Axle Annie*. Illustrated by Tedd Arnold. Dial, 1999.

Axle Annie is a bus driver who never fails to get the kids to school, even in the worst blizzards. This makes life miserable for Shifty Rhodes, another bus driver, who desperately wants school to be closed for a snow day. One day, the radio announces the school closings and mentions that only one school remains open, and that's—" 'Don't say Burskyville!' pleaded Shifty. 'Burskyville,' said the radio."

Pulver, Robin. *Mrs. Toggle's Zipper*. Illustrated by R. W. Alley. Simon & Schuster, 1990.

Mrs. Toggle's winter coat zipper gets stuck because the "thingamajig is missing from my zipper." The students try their best to pull her coat off, as does the school nurse and principal. The custodian finally comes up with a simple solution. Sequels: *Mrs. Toggle and the Dinosaur* (Simon & Schuster, 1991); *Mrs. Toggle's Beautiful Blue Shoe* (Simon & Schuster, 1991).

## SPECIAL EVENTS

Library programs billed as special events will often succeed in drawing both the regular library users and the kids who rarely visit the library. As long as the topic is intriguing, non-library users will take the time to find out what all the fuss is about. Once again, humor could be that draw. Many special events are planned around holidays and library campaigns, such as National Children's Book Week and Read Across America. The sample program Boo Ha-Ha! is aimed at children in grades 3-5 and combines humor with a yearly Halloween ghost stories session.

## *Boo Ha-Ha!*

Publicize this event as being only for grades 3-5. "Younger children will be turned away at the door." This little negative statement, usually a no-no for library publicity, can actually attract the target audience.

### ROOM DECORATIONS

Decorate the program area with a haunted-house setting, complete with fake cobwebs, jack-o'-lanterns, and dim lighting. In the past, I've had some of the best room decorations created by local scout troops. Set up a table with a colorful assortment of Halloween goodies for refreshments.

### ACTIVITIES

Set up another table near the refreshments for the popular game "Dead Man's Brains." Line up a series of small boxes. Cut a hole in each box, big enough so that kids can put their hands inside, but small enough so that they can't see what's inside. Place one of the following items in each box and label the boxes: Brains (really a fresh tomato), Eyes (two peeled grapes), Nose (chicken bone or small raw carrot), Ear (dried apricot), Hand (rubber glove filled with ice), Heart (raw liver), Blood (bowl of ketchup thinned with warm water), and The Worms That Ate Everything Else (cooked spaghetti noodles). Have a staff person or volunteer stand nearby so that the kids won't pull the items out of the boxes and start flinging them at each other. Again, I speak from experience.

Once everyone is settled, the storyteller, who should be dressed for the occasion, perhaps as a funeral director, can choose from a variety of humorous ghost stories.

### SOURCES

Baltuck, Naomi. *Crazy Gibberish and Other Story Hour Stretches.* Linnet, 1993.

> Baltuck has the best version of the traditional favorite known as "Red Lips." A scary visitor appears over the course of three nights and mumbles, "Do you know what I can do with these long, long fingers and these red, red lips?" For the punch line, the storyteller drums her fingers on her lips and goes "Bub-bub-bub-bub-bub." I usually change the story around to tell it in the first person as if it happened to me as a child.

Bennett, Jill. *Teeny Tiny*. Illustrated by Tomie DePaola. Putnam, 1985.

Kids love this story even though they've probably heard it a zillion times. There are many picture book versions on the market. I happen to like DePaola's artwork, even though this is an easy story to memorize and share without the book. Practice telling the story several times to get the timing down. When I say the final line, "Take it!" I not only increase my volume, I also lower my pitch. This adds to the comedy since the line is spoken by a little old lady. It helps to make the kids jump, too.

Cole, Joanna, and Stephanie Calmenson. *The Scary Book*. Morrow, 1991.

This book contains lighthearted versions of the traditional favorites "Taily-Po" and "The Viper," as well as several monster knock-knock jokes, riddles, and tongue twisters.

MacDonald, Margaret Read. *When the Lights Go Out: 20 Scary Stories to Tell*. Wilson, 1988.

Most of the stories in this collection aren't humorous, but MacDonald has a nice variation of "Bear Hunt" called "Let's Go on a Ghost Hunt." This activity will be a good chance to move around between stories. Even the older kids will get into it.

O'Malley, Kevin. *Velcome*. Walker, 1997.

Here's a good picture book to share with this age group. A creepy narrator reads several short, classic, traditional, not-so-scary, "scary" stories and jokes. He also shows the reader something so horrible you'll need to call your mommy (a plate of mixed vegetables). The narrator's dog adds to the fun by holding up a sign that warns the reader to stop reading.

Schwartz, Alvin. *In a Dark, Dark Room and Other Scary Stories*. Illustrated by Dirk Zimmer. HarperCollins, 1984.

The book's macabre humor is best demonstrated in the traditional story "The Green Ribbon." The female protagonist's head falls off when her husband unties the green ribbon around her neck. Bring a prop doll with a detachable head for the visual punch. Don't forget to tie a green ribbon around the doll's neck. The short poem "In the Graveyard" also always gets a laugh. Chant it as a quiet, mournful tune that will lull the audience before the big scream at the end.

Schwartz, Alvin. *Scary Stories to Tell in the Dark.* HarperCollins, 1981.

This extremely popular collection of scary stories contains several humorous stories, such as "The Viper," "The Hearse Song," "The Slithery-Dee," "The Ghost with the Bloody Fingers," "Old Woman All Skin and Bone," and "The Attic," in which the main character screams long and loud because he steps on a nail. Surprisingly, the story that gets the most laughs for me is "Me Tie Dough-Ty Walker." A boy and his dog spend the night in a haunted house. A voice outside chants the title phrase. The dog replies, "Lynchee kinchy colly molly dingo dingo." The kids in the audience find that hysterical. Eventually, a head falls down the chimney, the dog dies of fright, the head slowly turns toward the boy, and the storyteller jumps at someone in the audience and screams, "AAAAAAH!"

Schwartz, Alvin. *More Scary Stories to Tell in the Dark.* HarperCollins, 1984.

The next volume in Schwartz's series has a section of humorous scary stories titled "The Last Laugh." "The Brown Suit" describes a gross mix-up at a funeral parlor. "Bad News" is the funniest story because it contains a good news/bad news setup. A guy dies and returns to his friend as a ghost. The good news is that they play baseball in heaven. The bad news is that the living friend is scheduled to pitch tomorrow.

Schwartz, Alvin. *Scary Stories 3: More Tales to Chill Your Bones.* HarperCollins, 1991.

This collection also has a humor section titled "Whoooooooo?" Stories include "Stranger," "Is Something Wrong," "It's Him," and "T-H-U-P-P-P-P-P-P," a story similar to "Red Lips." In this story, the ghost puts its fingers in its ears, sticks out its tongue, and makes a raspberry noise.

Young, Richard, et al., eds. *Favorite Scary Stories of American Children.* August House, 1990.

This collection contains versions of several popular ghost stories, such as "Stop That Coffin," "Red Velvet Ribbon," and "Rap . . . Rap . . . Rap!"

Young, Richard, et al. *Scary Story Reader.* August House, 1993.

A section titled "Laugh Yourself to Death" contains versions of "The Viper" and "Bony Fingers," a version of "Red Lips." The funniest stories include "The Skeleton in the Closet," in which several kids and a janitor find the skeletal remains of the 1954 Hide-and-Seek Champion, and

"Bloody Fingers," in which a ghoul chases a kid. When he reaches the kid, he yells, "Tag! You're it!"

I adapt this story into a long narrative set in the library. I tell the kids I was working late, long after everyone else left. The ghoul chased me all over the stacks, the children's room, the bathrooms, and the offices. It gives me a chance, as the storyteller, to run around before clapping my hand on someone and saying the ghoul's punch line.

Sprinkle the program with poems, jokes, and riddles. Here are a few sources:

Adler, David. *The Twisted Witch and Other Spooky Riddles*. Illustrated by Victoria Chess. Holiday House, 1985.
Hall, Katy. *Creepy Riddles*. Illustrated by S. D. Schindler. Dial, 1998.
Kennedy, X. J. *Ghastlies, Goops, and Pincushions*. Illustrated by Ron Barrett. Margaret K. McElderry, 1989.
Phillips, Louis. *Haunted House Jokes*. Illustrated by James Marshall. Viking, 1987.
Sloat, Teri. *Really, Really Bad Monster Jokes*. Illustrated by Mike Wright. Candlewick, 1998.

## THEME PARTIES

Many libraries have had great success hosting Harry Potter theme parties at their libraries. Kids come dressed like characters from the books, and the library staff has related decorations, activities, and perhaps refreshments.

Librarians can use the same approach for theme parties based on humorous children's books. Begin by looking through the books to collect ideas that can be translated into party decorations and activities. Included are theme party outlines for the Wayside School series by Louis Sachar, the Captain Underpants series by Dav Pilkey, and the Time Warp Trio series by Jon Scieszka.

### *Wayside School Party*

Wayside School was erroneously built thirty stories high, one classroom stacked on top of another. The stories in the Wayside School series are based on Mrs. Jewls's classroom located on the thirtieth floor.

The Wayside books by Louis Sachar are: *Sideways Stories from Wayside School* (Knopf, 1978); *Wayside School Is Falling Down* (Lothrop, 1989);

*Sideways Arithmetic from Wayside School* (Scholastic, 1989); *Wayside School Gets a Little Stranger* (Morrow, 1995).

## ROOM DECORATIONS

Since you probably don't have free access to a thirty-story building, you can reenact the tall school in a single-floor space by hanging a few signs that read Left Side Up and Right Side Down. Hang a sign that reads Today's Special: Mushroom Surprise. Label the doors Goozack.

Place a large sheet of paper on the wall or a blackboard if you have one. Write the word *Discipline* on the board. Leave space for kids in the know to write their names and place a check mark, or circle their names. If you need to know why, read the books.

## REFRESHMENTS

Serve apples. Mrs. Gorf turns her students into apples before turning into one herself in the first chapter of the first Wayside book. Serve "baloneos." These are Oreo cookies with pieces of bologna in place of the white stuff in the middle. Have regular Oreo cookies on hand for the squeamish and the sensible. Fill a coffee container with Tootsie Roll Pops. Mrs. Jewls usually has such a container on her desk to reward students for their behavior and "correct" answers.

## ACTIVITIES

Have the children write their names on name tags as they arrive. When everyone is assembled, tell them to switch name tags with another person, much like Mrs. Jewls's students did when they had a substitute teacher.

Make PA announcements as Principal Kidswatter. You can welcome the kids with your own script or you can use Principal Kidswatter's hilarious lines from chapter 2 of *Wayside School Gets a Little Stranger.* Read the section from the first chapter of this book that starts with the sentence "But before you enter, you should know something about Wayside School." It will explain the whole nonsense of there not being a nineteenth floor and all.

Next, lead the kids in a sing-along of "Wayside School Is Falling Down" to the tune of "London Bridge Is Falling Down." The new words can be found in chapter 11 of *Wayside School Is Falling Down.*

Read three or four of your favorite chapters from the Wayside School books. My favorites are "Paul" from *Sideways Stories from Wayside School,* "A

Package for Mrs. Jewls" from *Wayside School Is Falling Down,* and "Poetry" from *Wayside School Gets a Little Stranger.* Instruct the kids to yell "Boo" when you finish each story, as they do when Louis the Yard Teacher tells stories.

Have the library staff act out a skit based on chapter 24 of *Sideways Stories from Wayside School.* Place two staff members on one side of your program area. They will act as Mrs. Jewls and a student named Dameon. Place a third staff member on the other side of the room to play Louis the Yard Teacher. Mrs. Jewls asks Dameon to run down all thirty floors and ask Louis if he'd like to watch a movie with the class. Louis asks which movie. Dameon runs up the thirty floors. Mrs. Jewls tells him. He runs down the thirty floors. Louis asks another question. Dameon runs back and forth several times. You can simulate Dameon running up and down by having the actor run in place and slowly creep from one end of the room to the other. Of course, Dameon soon runs out of breath. In the end, Mrs. Jewls informs him that the movie is already over.

Host a spelling contest. In the Wayside books, the children somehow spell synonyms of the words they're given to spell. When asked to spell "tired," one student recited, "Tired. S-L-E-E-P-Y. Tired." Another student was presented with "package." "Package. B-O-X. Package." After sharing these examples, hand your party-goers a thesaurus and have them spell a synonym for each word you give them.

Play "Pin the Pigtail on Leslie." In all three books, Paul torments poor Leslie for having pigtails. He always wants to pull them. Put up a poster with the back of Leslie's head drawn in. Blindfold the students and have them try to pin her pigtails to their correct location.

Create a jump-rope area. Post the words to the jump-rope chant listed in chapter 16 of *Wayside School Gets a Little Stranger* on the wall. Post another piece of paper on the wall and encourage your kids to name Mrs. Jewls's baby. Get them started by reading the names suggested in the book: Rainbow Sunshine, Bucket Head, Jet Rocket, and Cootie Face. Have a staff person write down the new names.

## Captain Underpants Party

Dav Pilkey's Captain Underpants books are very popular and controversial in some communities. This particular theme is for the brave, but here's a plan that's guaranteed to attract a crowd that comes dressed in the spirit of the event.

The Captain Underpants books are: *The Adventures of Captain Underpants* (Scholastic, 1997); *Captain Underpants and the Attack of the Talking Toilets* (Scholastic, 1999); *Captain Underpants and the Invasion of the Incredibly Naughty Cafeteria Ladies from Outer Space* (Scholastic, 1999); *Captain Underpants and the Perilous Plot of Professor Poopypants* (Scholastic, 2000); *Captain Underpants and the Wrath of the Wicked Wedgie Woman* (Scholastic, 2001); *The Captain Underpants Extra-Crunchy Book O' Fun* (Scholastic, 2001).

## ROOM DECORATIONS

Decorate the program area in the school colors: gray and dark gray. Place a Today's Menu sign on one wall. Cut several pieces of poster board and write weird words and phrases on each one. Put tape on the back of the pieces so that the kids can arrange them to create weird cafeteria offerings. Look through the Captain Underpants books for key words such as *fried, baked, octopus, eyeballs,* and *slime.*

## REFRESHMENTS

For treats, serve Mr. Krupp's Krispy Krupcakes (any kind of cupcake) and Anti-Evil Zombie Nerd Juice (any kind of juice).

## ACTIVITIES

As the kids enter the area, have them fill out name tags with the new silly names they received from Professor Poopypants's Name Change-O-Chart. The chart can be found in both *Captain Underpants and the Perilous Plot of Professor Poopypants* and *The Captain Underpants Extra-Crunchy Book O' Fun.* Kids will be instructed to follow a formula that transforms their names into new, silly names. By following the chart, for example, my name, Rob Reid, becomes Loopy Gizzardbuns. My editor's name, Karen Young, becomes Flunky Gorillapants, and my good friend, David Stoeri, becomes Gidget Pizzalips. Dav Pilkey's own name becomes Gidget Hamsterbrains.

*The Captain Underpants Extra-Crunchy Book O' Fun* contains several puzzles that can be reproduced for the event as well as a Mad-Lib story that participants can fill in as a group.

Hold a demonstration of a volcano powered by baking soda and vinegar, similar to the volcano in *Captain Underpants and the Invasion of the Incredibly*

*Naughty Cafeteria Ladies from Outer Space.* You can also make green slime mentioned in the same book. Instructions for making volcanoes and slime can be found in several science experiment books and web sites.

Since the two main characters in the Captain Underpants books are always drawing comics, you may want to invite an art teacher or local cartoonist to give a demonstration. A similar activity would be for participants to make their own flip books. Instructions can be found in *The Captain Underpants Extra-Crunchy Book O' Fun.* Pilkey's web site, www.pilkey.com, contains more games, jokes, and drawing activities.

Cap off the party by reading selections from the Captain Underpants books.

## The Time Warp Trio Party

Jon Scieszka's Time Warp Trio features three boys who travel back and forth in time with the aid of a magical book.

The Time Warp Trio series, published by Viking, includes: *Knights of the Kitchen Table* (1991); *The Not-So-Jolly Roger* (1991); *The Good, the Bad, and the Goofy* (1992); *Your Mother Was a Neanderthal* (1993); *2095* (1995); *Tut, Tut* (1996); *Summer Reading Is Killing Me* (1998); *It's All Greek to Me* (1999); *See You Later, Gladiator* (2000); *Sam Samurai* (2001).

**PUBLICITY**

Publicize the event as a costume party. Invite the kids to dress up as characters from the many time periods featured in the series. These include early humans, ancient civilizations (Chinese, Egyptian, Greek, Roman), European medieval times, pirates, cowboys/cowgirls, futuristic costumes, and costumes of characters in popular children's books.

**ACTIVITIES**

Set up stations to represent each of the books. Have an appropriate activity or refreshment at each station. Several of the books feature stunts the boys play, such as the Powerbroom trick from *The Good, the Bad, and the Goofy.* Use these stunts as activities at the stations. The Knights of the Kitchen Table station can have a black knight piñata since the boys strike the black knight with a stick in the book. At the Not-So-Jolly Roger station you can provide directions for a library treasure hunt or simply pass out coconut pieces or candy wrapped in gold foil. Have marker and paper for kids to create their own cave drawings at the Your Mother Was a Neanderthal station. Have kids at the 2095 station write down predictions for the future and put them in a time capsule. Brainstorm other activities and treats to use at the other stations.

Place a book decorated as The Book in the center of the room. Descriptions can be found in several Time Warp Trio books. When the children leave one station, they have to go to the center of the room, touch The Book, and "transport" to another station.

Since the boys in the book use magic as their means of transportation, and since one of the boys has a magician for an uncle, a performance by a magician is a perfect way to end the program.

# 4

## Humor Programs for Middle-School and High-School Students

It's tough to determine what's funny to this age group and what's not. I found that the simplest approach is to let the students develop the humor and share it as a library program. This combination of writing and performing works best when structured in a storytelling process. The librarian demonstrates various types of storytelling, the students use these demonstrations as models for their writing exercises, and then the students read or perform their creations for the public. The storytelling and writing program models included in this chapter are for a Liars' Club or Tall-Tale session, a wordplay celebration featuring spoonerisms, and a Finish The Story exercise. This chapter also has an outline for a non-writing program: a teen public reading billed as Comedy Club.

## STORYTELLING AND WRITING PROGRAMS

April is National Humor Month. Plan a teen humor program or series of programs to be presented during this time. Planning should start a few months in advance. Create a timetable. Contact area middle-school and high-school English teachers. Arrange for them to visit the library with their students or for you to visit their classrooms. Budget or solicit funds to publish student submissions as a small booklet.

Meet with the students a month or two before the public library presentation. Librarians need not worry about teaching writing skills. Simply share the storytelling models. Let the students and teachers work on the stories. As you end your visit, distribute fliers that describe the length of the submissions, rules, library contact names, instructions on how and where to submit the manuscripts, and deadlines. This is not a contest but a chance for students to share their creations with the community.

### Liars' Club

While meeting with the students, ask them to name a few famous tall-tale characters, such as Paul Bunyan or Pecos Bill. Show the students a few tall-tale books from the library and introduce them to some lesser-known tall-tale characters. Explain how these tall-tale heroes are associated with certain occupations. For example, Paul Bunyan was linked to the lumberjacks, Pecos Bill to cowboys, and Mike Fink to river folk. Explain that librarians have their own tall-tale hero and show them the picture book *Library Lil* by Suzanne Williams.

Have the students create a new tall-tale character during a brainstorming session. The new character should be a hero to students everywhere—a super-student. Give this character a name and exploits that are bigger than life. If someone states that the new character is so smart that he or she can get a 4.0 grade point average without studying, urge them to exaggerate this point even more. Have the tall-tale character achieve a 100.0 grade point average on a 4.0 scale. Introduce a nemesis for the hero—perhaps a particularly mean teacher. Instead of giving every student an automatic F, this teacher gives out Triple Zs. Ask the students and their teachers to develop more original tall-tale characters and submit them to the library.

Instead of tall-tale characters, students might wish to compile lists of whoppers for the Liars' Club. Tell or read the exaggerated stories found in Sid Fleischman's McBroom books (see page 116) or Alvin Schwartz's *Whoppers: Tall Tales and Other Lies*. String together several whoppers around a particular subject to create a big lie or a mini–tall tale. Since I'm from Wisconsin, I strung together several whoppers about cold winters and large mosquitoes. I call it "The Wisconsin Mini–Tall Tale."

> "It's cold in Wisconsin. Our state bird is the penguin. Last winter, we had to drill twenty feet into the ground just to read the thermometer. The mercury was jumping up and down in the bulb trying to get

warm. We saw two hound dogs pushing a jack rabbit just to jump-start it for the chase. Some people joke that Wisconsin has four seasons: winter, winter, winter, and winter. But that's just an exaggeration. Winter doesn't start until July 5 and only runs until the next July 3. The Fourth of July gets really, really hot, though. That's when the super big mosquitoes come out. Some folks put saddles on them and ride them at the local rodeo. Other folks form huge posses to grab mosquitoes as they fly by. Then they cut off the stingers with chain saws and sell them to the company that makes telephone poles. Mosquitoes today aren't as big as when I was a kid. Heard it's because the kids nowadays eat so much candy that the mosquitoes get cavities in their stingers. Hey! Here comes a good-sized one now. Where's my chain saw?"

Encourage the students to do some research through the folklore section of the library and string along their own whoppers. Schwartz's Whoppers book has an extensive bibliography of old sources. When all submissions are in, invite the students to read their works to the public. Cap off the evening with a performance by a storyteller who specializes in tall tales.

## Spoonerisms

A similar program involves the creation of spoonerisms. Spoonerisms involve swapping parts of words. Spoonerisms often get the biggest laughs from audiences. Even if the audience can't catch all of the tag lines, they laugh at the nonsensical sounds.

It's very hard to find spoonerisms in print, so I've included three original ones as models. Share them with the students and then ask them to create their own. Instruct them to write an outline of a well-known story and look for key phrases that can be changed around. Play around with popular words and phrases. Feel free to stray from the traditional story line to go for the laughs. A thesaurus is a handy tool to use when creating spoonerisms. Don't try to change every word or phrase. The audience needs to hear some normal-sounding words for context. And yes, the students will create some inappropriate and vulgar combinations. Acknowledge ahead of time that this will happen, and ask them to keep these to themselves.

Spoonerisms are hard to write, but they are worth the effort. If the writing aspect doesn't appeal to you, you can read the following spoonerisms, distribute print copies afterward, and have the students translate them. I've retained the sounds of the newly created spoonerisms but have altered some of the spelling for easier reading.

*Introduction:* "Have you ever been pickled tink? Have you ever felt like a billion mucks? Did you know that the waste is a terrible thing to mind? Well then, you just might be in the right frame of mind for some spoonerisms!"

### "Little Rude Riding Head"

Once atime upon, a gritty little pearl named Little Rude Riding Head had a gasket for her branny.
She had . . .

   . . . a broaf of homemade lead,

   . . . a wottle of bine,

   . . . grapples and apes,

   . . . three or four belly jeans,

   . . . a bag of pollilops,

   . . . some shop chewey,

   . . . a twelve-inch peese chizza

   . . . some sicken noodle choop,

   . . . some plack-eyed bees,

   . . . and a bottle of boot rear.

On the way, she met a wolfy wile.

   . . . He was cotton to the roar.

   . . . He was a party-smants and a skunky stink.

   . . . He was a real snattle-rake.

   . . . He was the shack bleep of the family.

The wolf tooted through the skimbers while Red walked at a pail's snace.
Granny was all bin and skones, but choosers can't be beggy.
The wolf chicked his lops and burped the old gal down in one slight.
Granny found herself in that belly wolf's smelly.
He stuck her kite nap on his head and beeped into led.
Red arrived and said, "What pig beepers you have."
The wolf said, "All the setter to be you, you tweet little sing."
Red said, "What a hig bonker you have."

The wolf said, "All the smetter to bell you, punny high."
Red said, "What lig bips you have."
The wolf said, " Weed them and reap!"
Suddenly, there was a dot in the shark!
A hassing punter saved the day!
And they all happed lively after.
All except for the wolf, who learned that humans
"Stick softly and carry a big speak."

Translation:

## "Little Red Riding Hood"

One upon a time, a pretty little girl named Little Red Riding Hood had
   a basket for her granny.
She had . . .

> . . . a loaf of homemade bread,
> . . . a bottle of wine,
> . . . apples and grapes,
> . . . three or four jelly beans,
> . . . a bag of lollipops,
> . . . some chop suey,
> . . . a twelve-inch cheese pizza,
> . . . some chicken noodle soup,
> . . . some black-eyed peas,
> . . . and a bottle of root beer.

On the way, she met a wily wolf.

> . . . He was rotten to the core.
> . . . He was a smarty-pants and a stinky skunk.
> . . . He was a real rattlesnake.
> . . . He was the black sheep of the family.

The wolf scooted through the timbers while Red walked at a snail's
   pace.
Granny was all skin and bones, but beggars can't be choosy.
The wolf licked his chops and slurped the old gal down in one bite.
Granny found herself in that smelly wolf's belly.

He stuck her nightcap on his head and leaped into bed.
Red arrived and said, "What big peepers you have."
The wolf said, "All the better to see you, you sweet little thing."
Red said, "What a big honker you have."
The wolf said, "All the better to smell you, honey pie."
Red said, "What big lips you have."
The wolf said, "Read them and weep!"
Suddenly, there was a shot in the dark!
A passing hunter saved the day!
And they all lived happily ever after.
All except for the wolf, who learned that humans
"Speak softly and carry a big stick."

### "Bean and the Jackstalk"

Once atime upon, Jack lived with his mold other.
She called him a bazy loans.
She told him, "A waste is a terrible thing to mind."
So, Jack cold his sow for bean threes.
They were bagical means.
They were the greatest bing since sliced thread.
Jack's mold other was mopping had.
She stew her black and bossed the teens.
That night, a great stalkbean grew clouder than the highs.
Jack hooted up the stalk and skid in the cupboard.
He was as bug as a rug in a snug.
Then, Jack stole a gag of bold that belonged to a giant.
I mean, this guy was a mall tan.
. . . He was a really fried weak.
. . . He was a floated bellow.
. . . A befty hulk.
. . . Bat and furly.
. . . He was one wig bopper.
Jack grabbed a harp and chooted a licken that could gay olden legs.
The grover-own mammoth woke up.
Jack said, "Don't cry over milked spill."
The giant said, "I'll bind your groans to break my med!"
Jack beaned the chopstalk and the fig bellow did a felly blop.
He was doored as a deadnail.

Jack gold the sold and they all happed lively after ever.
All except for the mumbo jonster.

Translation:

### "Jack and the Beanstalk"

Once upon a time, Jack lived with his old mother.
She called him a lazybones.
She told him, "A mind is a terrible thing to waste."
So, Jack sold his cow for three beans.
They were magical beans.
They were the greatest thing since sliced bread.
Jack's old mother was hopping mad.
She blew her stack and tossed the beans.
That night, a great beanstalk grew higher than the clouds.
Jack scooted up the stalk and hid in the cupboard.
He was as snug as a bug in a rug.
Then, Jack stole a bag of gold that belonged to a giant.
I mean, this guy was a tall man.
. . . He was a really wide freak.
. . . He was a bloated fellow.
. . . A hefty bulk.
. . . Fat and burly.
. . . He was one big whopper.
Jack grabbed the harp and looted a chicken that could lay golden eggs.
The overgrown mammoth woke up.
Jack said, "Don't cry over spilt milk."
The giant said, "I'll grind your bones and make my bread!"
Jack chopped the beanstalk and the big fellow did a
    belly flop.
He was dead as a doornail.
Jack sold the gold and they all lived happily ever after.
All except for the jumbo monster.

### "Goldibear and the Three Locks"

Once atime upon, there was Boppa Pear, Bommy Mare, and the Beeny
    Weeny Tear.

One morning, their hop was too slot.
Boppa Pear said, "Ow! I've turnt my bung!"
So they went for a skittle lip in the woods.
Soon, there was a dock at the nor.
It was a gritty little pearl named Loldigocks.
To make a short story long, she basically dashed the trump.
Finally, she said, "I could use a snittle looze."
She sent to weep.
She even snarted to store.
When they arrived home, the shurry fammals were mocked.
Boppa Pear said, "Somebody's been oating my eatmeal!"
Bommy Mare said, "Somebody's been pouring my eatidge!"
And the Beeny Weeny Tear said, "Somebody's been souping
   my slurp!"
They found the chusted bares and headed for the red booms.
Boppa Pear said, "Somebody's been bedding in my nap!"
Bommy Mare said, "Somebody's been taking a natcap in my bed!"
And the Beeny Weeny Tear said, "Somebody's been beeping in
   my sled!"
The bears copped the calls and they all happed livily after ever.
All except for the little smart goldy pants.


Translation:

### "Goldilocks and the Three Bears"

Once upon a time, there was Papa Bear, Mommy Bear, and the
   Teeny Weeny Bear.
Once morning, their slop was too hot.
Papa Bear said, "Ow! I've burnt my tongue!"
So they went for a little skip in the woods.
Soon, there was a knock at the door.
It was a pretty little girl named Goldilocks.
To make a long story short, she basically trashed the dump.
Finally, she said, "I could use a little snooze."
She went to sleep.
She even started to snore.
When they arrived home, the furry mammals were shocked.
Papa Bear said, "Somebody's been eating my oatmeal!"

Mommy Bear said, "Somebody's been eating my porridge!"
And the Teeny Weeny Bear said, "Somebody's been slurping
    my soup!"
They found their busted chairs and headed for the bedrooms.
Papa Bear said, "Somebody's been napping in my bed!"
Mommy Bear said, "Somebody's been taking a catnap in my bed!"
And the Teeny Weeny Bear said, "Somebody's been sleeping in
    my bed!"
The bears called the cops and they all lived happily
    ever after.
All except for the little gold smarty pants.

### Finish the Story

Here are two more short writing exercises that can be turned into public performances at the library.

1. *The Book of Bad Ideas* by Laura Huliska-Beith (Little, Brown, 2000) contains several one-line "bad ideas" accompanied by illustrations. Examples of bad ideas include "keeping your glue stick and lip balm in the same pocket" and "asking your friend to give you a quick haircut on Class Picture Day." Have students write more "bad ideas."

2. Ask the students to write answering machine messages that feature songs or book titles. Here are several examples written by Ann Shuda, one of my former graduate students, and her family.

"Hello. It is TUESDAY, JUNE 29TH, 1999. We are not in right now. Dan went to THE GREAT BALL GAME with the SIX CHINESE BROTHERS IN COAL COUNTRY WHERE ONCE THERE WAS A WOOD. Afterward he will WATCH THE STARS COME OUT while playing NIGHT GOLF with GEORGE AND MARTHA DOWN BY THE POND.

Ann is at a cooking class learning HOW TO MAKE AN APPLE PIE AND SEE THE WORLD using SWEET DRIED APPLES FOR THE VERY LAST FIRST TIME for SPOT'S BIRTHDAY PARTY in CHATO'S KITCHEN. Later, she will go IN THE NIGHT KITCHEN with BRAVE IRENE and make pies out of EACH PEACH PEAR PLUM, THE FIRST STRAWBERRIES, THE RUNAWAY BUNNY, and BLUEBERRIES FOR SAL. They will also make STONE SOUP in an EMPTY POT using ONE GRAIN OF RICE, THE MYSTERIOUS TADPOLE, and RECHENKA'S EGGS.

Bethany is playing her harp at MISS SPIDER'S WEDDING ON GRANDMA'S ROOF with MUFARO'S BEAUTIFUL DAUGHTERS, the SONG AND DANCE MAN, and THE PIANO MAN. They are playing LIZARD'S SONG while ANGELINA BALLERINA IS DANCING WITH THE INDIANS.

Allie, who is shooting baskets—SWISH!—is one step closer to ALLIE'S BASKETBALL DREAM. You can catch her at the mall in the afternoon. She took LILY'S PURPLE PLASTIC PURSE. It must be MARKET DAY. They have CAPS FOR SALE. I hope she doesn't buy TWO OF EVERYTHING. Tonight, we are taking her NIGHT DRIVING so she can take her driving test WHEN SUMMER ENDS.

ONE-EYED JAKE is planting THE CARROT SEED IN GRANDPA'S GARDEN with JOHN HENRY and FREDERICK. He is going over to ARTHUR'S FIRST SLEEPOVER tonight. It's always fun when IRA SLEEPS OVER. He hopes he doesn't have to sleep next to Bootsie. BOOTSIE BARKER BITES. I hope he remembered to bring his TOPS AND BOTTOMS. He was happy to be invited because NOTHING EVER HAPPENS ON OUR BLOCK.

Rosie went for a walk to MCELLIGOT'S POOL with BEA AND MR. JONES. If it is too crowded, she will go to HEN LAKE or TAR BEACH. She is leaving tonight with MADELINE. They are taking an AIRPLANE RIDE to THE GREAT KAPOK TREE. They will go to the COLOR ZOO, PETER SPIER'S CIRCUS, and then take some PICKLES TO PITTSBURGH. They will be gone for MANY MOONS.

Please leave a message at the beep.

# READING PROGRAM

## Comedy Club

It's a challenge to find humorous young adult literature. Many of the books that the reviews list as "hilarious" and "rollicking" still fall short. Many young adult books have humorous moments, but the humor doesn't hold up throughout the entire book. That's why Comedy Club was created—to seek out those few moments and to locate other humorous material that will interest teens.

Comedy Club is simply a reading program. Many libraries hold readings for poetry, author visits, and special occasions, such as Banned Books Week. Why not sponsor a humor reading program? Encourage local teens to sign up to read. Help them scour the library stacks to find material that appeals to them and their peers.

## SOURCES

Coville, Bruce. "Am I Blue?" In *Am I Blue? Coming Out from the Silence,* edited by Marion Dane Bauer. HarperCollins, 1994.

The title story from this collection of short stories describes a fairy godfather who helps a young teen learn about society's various, and sometimes hypocritical, attitudes toward gays.

Crutcher, Chris. "A Brief Moment in the Life of Angus Bethune." In *Athletic Shorts.* Greenwillow, 1991.

Read the first half of this short story as Angus comments on his parents, his size, and his name.

Lynch, Chris. *Slot Machine.* HarperCollins, 1995.

Elvin resists being slotted into a sport at his school's summer program. Read selected letters that he writes home to his mother.

Paulsen, Gary. *Harris and Me.* Harcourt, 1993.

The narrator describes a very wild summer on his cousin's farm. Read the first half of chapter 8 when the two boys play cowboys and jump on Bill the horse.

Paulsen, Gary. *The Schernoff Discoveries.* Delacorte, 1997.

Harold tries to explain the trials of adolescence as scientific theories. Read the second half of chapter 2, where Harold enacts revenge on the football team by dosing them with forty-three boxes of chocolate-flavored laxative. Also, read the second half of chapter 3, where Harold methodically tries to kiss his date and winds up with his tongue in her nostril.

Rennison, Louise. *Angus, Thongs, and Full-Frontal Snogging: Confessions of Georgia Nicolson.* HarperCollins, 2000.

Georgia is a fourteen-year-old British girl with a wild outlook on her life. Read her diary entries from Thursday, August 27, when she starts plucking her eyebrows and winds up shaving them both off. Sequels: *On the Bright Side, I'm Now the Girlfriend of a Sex God: Further Confessions of Georgia Nicolson* (HarperCollins, 2001); *Knocked Out by My Nunga-Nungas: Further, Further Confessions of Georgia Nicolson* (HarperCollins, 2002).

Supplement the Comedy Club reading with books marketed to adults that appeal to teens. Favorite authors include Douglas Adams, Bill Bryson, and Dave Barry. Look at books written by stand-up comedians such as Jerry Seinfeld and Ellen DeGeneres. Don't overlook Dorothy Parker, James Thurber, and Robert Benchley.

Keep the reading simple, and have fun with it. There's nothing quite like a library filled with laughing teens.

# 5

## Reader's Theater

Humorous stories come alive through reader's theater presentations. Students of all ages can get involved in this activity. Older students can help select material to adapt, develop the scripts, and present a library program for younger children. The older students like being able to perform without having to memorize a script. They can read from the script, a security blanket, so to speak. The younger children love to listen to these live presentations. Reader's theater is similar to reading aloud in that the listeners get to "see" the characters and actions in their minds as they hear the story.

Many of the picture books, easy readers, folklore, and even the poetry collections listed throughout this book are good sources to adapt into reader's theater productions. Look for books heavy on dialogue. If there is a lot of narration that is vital to the story, divide these lines among several readers. Author Aaron Shepard has a wonderful web site for script development and presentation tips, www.aaronshep.com. He also has a book titled *Stories on Stage: Scripts for Reader's Theater* (Wilson, 1993).

Other strong sources for reader's theater script development are *Reader's Theatre for Young Adults* (1989) and *Reader's Theatre for Children: Scripts and Development* (1990), both written by Kathy Howard Latrobe and Mildred Knight Laughlin and published by Teacher Ideas Press.

Children's author Margie Palatini was kind enough to grant permission to print this adaptation of her picture book *The Web Files*.

## The Web Files
### By Margie Palatini

### Cast of Characters

| | | |
|---|---|---|
| Web | Hen | Sheep |
| Bill | Little Boy Blue | Dirty Rat |
| Rooster | Horse | |

| | |
|---|---|
| WEB:<br>(*read like* Dragnet) | 6:32 A.M. This is the farm. My partner, Bill, and I were working the barnyard shift. It was peaceful. Quiet. Then we got the call. |
| ROOSTER: | Cock-a-doodle-doo! A lot of squawking going on down in the coop area, Ducktective Web. Looks like fowl play. Report says feathers are flying. Chief says we should check out the chicks. |
| WEB: | Chicks? |
| ROOSTER: | Check. |
| WEB: | Let's fly. |
| ALL:<br>(Dragnet *theme*) | Dum-De-Dum-Dum. |
| WEB: | 6:35 A.M. The hen's house. We knocked on the door. She answered. |
| HEN: | P'awk! P-p-p-awk! P'awk! P'awk! |
| WEB: | Just the facts, ma'am. Just the facts. |
| HEN: | I've been robbed! Robbed, I tell you. Robbed! Robbed! Robbed! |
| WEB: | So you're saying that you were robbed, is that right ma'am? What exactly is missing from the nest, ma'am? Eggs, ma'am? Chick, ma'am? |
| HEN: | P-p-peppers. |
| WEB: | Peppers? |
| HEN: | My perfect purple peppers that were just about ready to be pickled. |

| | |
|---|---|
| WEB: | About how many perfect purple almost-pickled peppers would you say were pilfered, pinched, and picked? A bushel? |
| HEN: | P'wak! P'wak! No—a peck! A peck, I tell you! A whole purple-pepper-pickin'-peck! |
| WEB: | Have any idea who would pick a peck of your perfect purple almost-pickled peppers? |
| HEN: | Not a clue. |
| WEB: | I turned to Bill and gave a quick quack. "Round up the usual suspects." |
| ALL: | Dum-De-Dum-Dum. |
| WEB: | 9:06 A.M. Headquarters was hopping. A miss named Muffet had just been tossed off her tuffet, and a gal named Peep was missing some sheep. I noticed that three little kittens had lost their mittens. They began to cry. I wanted to help, but I couldn't. I had pickled peppers to worry about. We had Horner in the corner and were trying to make Little Boy Blue quack. "Okay, Blue Boy. Quit blowing your horn. Time to make hay. Suppose you just tell me where you were this morning." |
| LITTLE BOY BLUE: | I'm innocent, I tell you! Innocent! I was under the haystack. Fast asleep! Honest. Ask anybody. |
| WEB: | Sure. Sure. I've heard that bedtime story before. Got any witnesses? |
| BILL: | No. The sheep were in the meadow. Cows were in the corn. |
| WEB: | Things looked black for the boy in blue. Then we got another call. |
| BILL: | There's been some horsin' around reported down near Barn and Pen. Looks like another robbery. |
| ALL: | Dum-De-Dum-Dum. |
| WEB: | 10:43 A.M. Corner of Barn and Pen. Bill and I talked to the horses. "Whoa! Whoa! You there. I'd like to ask a few questions if you don't mind, sir." |

| | |
|---|---|
| HORSE: | Na-a-a-ay. Not at all. |
| WEB: | What do you know about a peck of unlawfully picked perfect purple almost-pickled peppers? |
| HORSE: | Peppers? Peppers? A peck of purple peppers? Not a thing. But somebody just hightailed it out of here with a tub of my tartest tasty tomahtoes! |
| WEB: | Tomatoes? |
| HORSE: | You say to-may-toes, I say to-mah-toes. Somebody just hauled the whole thing off! |
| SHEEP: | And find my lettuce while you're at it, too. Somebody just lifted a load of my luscious leafy lettuce not ten minutes ago! This is ba-a-a-d! Really ba-a-d! |
| WEB: | My partner looked at me and scratched his head. |
| BILL: | Peppers? Tomatoes? Lettuce? What do you make out of all this, Web? |
| WEB: | There was only one thing to make out of all this. Salad. |
| ALL: | Dum-De-Dum-Dum. |
| WEB: | 11:47 A.M. My partner and I were still trying  to quack the case, but we didn't have any idea whom to ID. |
| BILL: | Rats! |
| WEB: | That's it! There was only one suspect who was sneaky enough and tricky enough to pick a peck of perfect purple almost-pickled peppers, take a tub of tasty tart tomatoes, and lift a load of lucious leafy lettuce. 12:22 P.M. My partner and I were hot on the trail of . . . that Dirty Rat. |
| ALL: | Dum-De-Dum-Dum. |
| WEB: | 12:46 P.M. A real hole in the wall. "We know you're holed up in there, you Dirty Rat. Let us in." He did. |
| DIRTY RAT: | Eh, what's up, Duck? |
| WEB: | There's been some trouble down on the farm. What do you know about a rash of recent robberies? |
| DIRTY RAT: | Robberies? Robberies? What makes you think I know anything about a robbery? I'm no cheesy snitch. |

| | |
|---|---|
| WEB: | Can it, Ratzo. You've been in nothing but garbage for years. |
| DIRTY RAT: | Okay. Sure. Go ahead, flatfoot. Look anywhere you want. But make it quick, Quacker—you're interrupting my lunch. |
| WEB: | Lunch, eh, Rodent? |
| DIRTY RAT: | Hey, what's going on here? You're not going to pin this rap on me. Where's your evidence, you waddling webfoot? You got nothing on me. Nothing, see? I'm clean. Clean, I tell you. Clean! |
| WEB: | I picked a piece of lettuce from under his chin. "Not clean enough, you Dirty Rat." I smelled his breath. Just as I suspected. Garlic mayo. "Book him, Ducko. His salad days are over." |
| DIRTY RAT: | Over? Over? But they can't be over! I haven't even had my dessert! |
| BILL: | Looks like you quacked another one, Web. But how did you ever figure out it was him? |
| WEB: | I just played a hunch that he ate the evidence for lunch . . . and forgot to use his napkin and brush his teeth. He's a dirty rat. He never did have good hygiene. |
| ALL: | Dum-De-Dum-Dum. |
| WEB: | The Dirty Rat was tried and convicted on three counts of vegetable vagrancy, offensive bad breath, and not using a napkin to wipe under his chin. He was sent up the river and was sentenced to six months of farm labor with time off for good behavior, better table manners, and clean teeth. Case closed. |
| ALL: | Dum-De-Dum-Dum. <br> Dum-De-Dum-Dum-Dum! |

# 6

# Lively Library Tours
# and School Visits

## TOUR SCRIPT

The following model tour script was inspired by "Class Visit Shortcuts," an article by Alice Hoffman and Mary Somerville (*School Library Journal*, December, 1982; 32). It helped me devise a humorous routine for visiting groups that's a welcome change from dreary, pointing tours.

LIBRARIAN: "Knock-knock."

CHILDREN: "Who's there?"

LIBRARIAN: "Boo."

CHILDREN: "Boo who?"

LIBRARIAN: "Oh, please don't be sad about visiting the library! It's one of the coolest places in town. We have a lot of great things to check out and all kinds of incredible information. Every day we help people find answers to all kinds of questions.

*(Give examples)*

"We can usually find the answers, but I'm having trouble with this question: If a doctor doctors another doctor, is the doctored doctor doctored the way the doctoring doctor wants to doctor the doctor, or is the doctored doctor doctored the way the doctored doctor wants to be doctored?

"As I mentioned before, we have a lot of books, magazines, and videos that you can check out. All you need is a library card that looks like this.

*(Hold up a library card)*

"We had a man in here the other day who lost his card. We're still trying to reach him."

*(Hold up an oversized facsimile of a library card issued to "P. Bunyan" and mounted on foam core board)*

The opening dialogue above sets the tone for fun. Now move over to the reference section. Hold up a copy of the *Guinness Book of World Records* and inform your listeners that the longest overdue library book was 288 years. Calculate how much money that would be according to your library's overdue policy. Skip over the replacement cost of the item and exaggerate the daily fine amount. For example, if your library charges a dime a day per item, multiply that by 365 days and then 288 years. The result is $10,512. Tell them "that's one record you shouldn't try to break." Ignore the kids if they protest that they won't live that long.

When you've covered the basics of library usage, move on to individual sections that play to your interests and strengths. I like to show the kids the cookbook area and tell them, "There's a little-known law that states that any kid who cooks something from a library's copy of a cookbook is required to bring a sample for the children's librarian." I'm still waiting for that first piece, but the line gets a lot of laughs. Some kids ask, "Really?"

Tell them whoppers from the folklore section: "It was soo-ooo cold I dropped my comb, and when I picked it up, the teeth were chattering." Put on a pair of nose-glasses and tell them jokes and riddles from the joke book section: "What goes 'buzz-a-choo, buzz-a-choo?' A bee with a cold." Wear a sports hat to show the location of the sports books. Show a craft you made from one of the craft books or a science experiment to promote science books. Perform a simple trick to highlight the magic books. Do an impression of a celebrity from the biography section.

You can use the same techniques to show off the fiction area. Your magic trick can highlight a fantasy book. Scour novelty shops for items that you might be able to connect to a particular book or category of books. A set of plastic vampire teeth could be used to promote nonfiction books on films, monsters, and dental hygiene, or for fiction such as *Bunnicula* by Deborah and James Howe, or *Bunny Money* by Rosemary Wells.

## *Five Tips for a Memorable Tour*

1. Read a short selection from any book listed in this book. Several people will usually try to check out your selection.

2. Surprise them by pointing out an ordinary object in the library: "Ladies and gentlemen, a library wastebasket!"

3. Unless the teacher requests it, never include a detailed explanation of the Dewey decimal system or other library lessons in your talk.

4. Distribute a flier that lists upcoming library events appropriate for their age, a joke or two, and a short list of funny books.

5. Close the tour with one of the library raps or closings from chapter 7 of this book.

## SCHOOL VISITS

Whether you're promoting your local summer library program or a nationwide campaign such as National Library Card Sign-Up Month, National Children's Book Week, National Library Week, or Read Across America, try to deliver a short, snappy program. Whether you're addressing single classrooms or large group assemblies, humor will make your visit memorable.

You can employ many of the tactics you use for a library tour when you visit students at their schools. I begin by introducing myself and telling them I'm from the public library. Then I tell them I almost didn't make it to their school. To illustrate why, I recite and act out "True Story" by Shel Silverstein from *Where the Sidewalk Ends*. The poem describes larger-than-life things that happen to the narrator, such as stepping into quicksand, being tied up in a cave, and dropped into a boiling lake.

Then I move into an audience participation story. I like to alternate between the traditional story "Sody Salleratus" (you can find a nifty version in my book *Family Storytime*) and (since you already purchased this book) my adaptation of the folktale "The Turnip," titled "The Biggest, Juiciest Apple in the Whole Orchard." I narrate the story and direct volunteers from the audience to act it out. I select kids from the different grade levels and ask a teacher or the principal to play the apple tree. The tree holds out its arms for the branches. The animal characters line up off to the side. One by one, they move to the tree and view an imaginary apple hanging from one of the branches. I make sure their eyes grow wide and their jaws truly drop before proceeding. They pull on the imaginary apple and they pull on each other while the audience recites, "They pulled and they pulled and they pulled." At the end of the story, they all take a bow.

### "The Biggest, Juiciest Apple in the Whole Orchard"
By Rob Reid

The biggest, juiciest apple in the whole orchard started as a small,
   pink blossom.
It grew as big as a coconut.
It grew as big as a bowling ball.
It grew as big as a watermelon.
It grew and grew and grew until it was as big as the tree itself.
It was the biggest, juiciest apple in the whole orchard.

A pig named Plump was rooting around the orchard.
He saw the apple.
His eyes grew wide. His jaw dropped.
That must be the biggest, juiciest apple in the whole orchard," he
   said.
"I want it!"
Plump the Pig grabbed the apple.
He pulled and pulled and pulled.
The tree bent over a tiny bit, but the apple stuck tight to the branch.

A goat named Gump was grubbing around the orchard.
She saw the apple.
Her eyes grew wide. Her jaw dropped.
"That must be the biggest, juiciest apple in the whole orchard," she
   said.
"I want it!"
Plump the Pig said, "I saw it first.
But I guess there's enough for both of us."
Gump the Goat pulled Plump the Pig.
Plump the Pig pulled the apple.
They pulled and pulled and pulled.
The tree bent over a little more, but the apple stuck tight to the
   branch.

A llama named Lump strolled in from a nearby llama farm.
She saw the apple.
Her eyes grew wide. Her jaw dropped.
"That must be the biggest, juiciest apple in the whole orchard," she
    said.
"I want it!"
Plump the Pig and Gump the Goat said, "We saw it first.
But we guess there's enough for all of us."
Lump the Llama pulled Gump the Goat.
Gump the Goat pulled Plump the Pig.
Plump the Pig pulled the apple.
They pulled and pulled and pulled.
The tree bent over a bit more, but the apple stuck tight to the
    branch.

A horse named Hunk was horsing around the orchard.
He saw the apple.
His eyes grew wide. His jaw dropped.
"That must be the biggest, juiciest apple in the whole orchard,"
    he said.
"I want it!"
Plump the Pig, Gump the Goat, and Lump the Llama said, "We saw
    it first.
But we guess there's enough for all of us."

Hunk the Horse pulled Lump the Llama.
Lump the Llama pulled Gump the Goat.
Gump the Goat pulled Plump the Pig.
Plump the Pig pulled the apple.
They pulled and pulled and pulled.
The tree bent over quite a bit, but the apple stuck tight to the
    branch.

A worm named Wimp was wiggling around the orchard.
She saw the apple.
Her eyes grew wide. Her jaw dropped.
"That must be the biggest, juiciest apple in the whole orchard,"
    she said.
"I want it!"

Plump the Pig, Gump the Goat, Lump the Llama, and Hunk the
   Horse said, "We saw it first. Go away. You're too tiny to help."
Wimp the Worm said, "Nonsense. I can help. There's enough for all
   of us."

So Wimp the Worm pulled Hunk the Horse.
Hunk the Horse pulled Lump the Llama.
Lump the Llama pulled Gump the Goat.
Gump the Goat pulled Plump the Pig.
Plump the Pig pulled the apple.
They pulled and pulled and pulled.
The tree bent all the way to the ground, but the apple stuck tight to
   the branch.

While they were pulling, Plump the Pig, Gump the Goat, Lump the
   Llama, and Hunk the Horse said, "We told you that you were too
   tiny to help. Scram!"
Wimp the Worm let go.
The tree snapped in the other direction and sent Plump the Pig,
Gump the Goat, Lump the Llama, and Hunk the Horse flying through the
   air and out of sight.
The tree snapped back.
The apple tore free from the branch and flew straight up into the air.
The apple did an apple turnover high overhead and headed straight
   for Wimp the Worm.
Wimp's eyes grew wide. Her jaw dropped.
She dug a hole in the ground and disappeared moments before the
   apple landed with a loud plop.
Wimp the Worm was trapped.
Did she worry? Did she fret? No!
She simply smiled and began to chew.
She chewed and chewed and chewed and chewed.
She said, "I guess there's enough for me."
And she was very, very happy for a long, long time
   Inside the biggest, juiciest apple in the whole orchard.

After the story, I briefly mention the purpose of my visit. My friend
Marge Loch-Wouters, who is a youth services librarian and the funniest
woman in the state of Wisconsin, warns librarians not to explain all the

details of how to get a library card or how to enroll in the summer reading program. That will kill the humor in a hurry. Keep these visits fun and memorable. The students can learn the rules at the library. Your job is to get them interested and to lead them to the library like the Pied Piper.

I end the school visit with a rap or another of the closings listed in chapter 7. Here are two alternative musical activities I sometimes include.

### "The Stinky Cheese Man Song"
#### By Krista Falteisek

(To *The Beverly Hillbillies* theme song)
Here's a story that I'm gonna tell.
My main goal is this book I want to sell.
When I'm through I hope that you will see,
That I have done this quite cleverly.
The Stinky Cheese Man, that is,
And other fairly stupid tales.
Listen closely now!

(Switch to *Gilligan's Island* theme song)
Just sit right back and you'll hear a tale,
A tale of Chicken Licken,
Who thought the sky was falling down
When the clouds began to thicken.
The first was Ducky Lucky,
And Goosey Loosey next.
They set off running right on down to tell the president.
To tell the president.

(Switch to *The Brady Bunch* theme song)
Here's a story of Cinderella,
Who was living with two stepsisters and mom.
They were four women living all together, but didn't get along.
Then one day Cinderella met Rumpelstiltskin,
And they knew that it was much more than a hunch,
That these two must somehow form a title,
That is how they became Cinderumpelstiltskin,

Cinderumpelstiltskin, Cinderumpelstiltskin,
That is how they became Cinderumpelstiltskin.

(Switch to *The Fintstones* theme song)
Stinky, Stinky Cheese Man,
He was made out of loneliness.
Popped out of an oven,
Ran away and became a pest.
No one really wanted him around.
Was the case with everyone he found.
Stinky, Stinky Cheese Man.
Have a fun time reading,
The Stinky Cheese Man
And Other Fairly Stupid Tales.

This next camp song was taught to me by a group of fifth-grade girls when I went to their school. I include it for any brave souls who encounter similar groups.

### "Tom the Toad"

*Chorus:*

O' Tom the Toad.
O' Tom the Toad.
Why did you hop onto the road?

You were my friend and now you're dead
You bear the marks of tire tread.

You did not see yon passing car
And now you're stretched out on the tar.
    (*Chorus*)

You didn't see the Subaru
Until it had run over you.

You hopped out on the yellow line
And turned into a streak of slime.
    (*Chorus*)

It's clear to all you're in a rut
We all did see your gushing gut.

You used to hop from place to place
And now your feet can touch your face.
    (*Chorus*)

You used to hop without a care
And now your guts are everywhere.

It wasn't your fault you couldn't hear
And now you're stuck on a Goodyear.
    (*Chorus*)

# 7

## Raps and Closings

I've also composed original rap lyrics to help me connect with kids. They create a humorous tone and bring welcome attention to the library. Feel free to use any of the following raps to promote your library. You can change the rap to fit your name: "I'm Rappin' Sue and you know what I do." Or change the opening lines to something more generic: "I'm a rappin' guy and you know why I like to tell kids about books," or "I'm a rappin' gal and I'm your pal and I like tellin' kids about books."

### "The Rappin' Rob Library Rap"
### (aka "The Library Rap")

By Rob Reid

I'm Rappin' Rob and I gotta job and that's tellin' kids about books.
So lend me an ear, get over here! And don't give me no dirty looks.
I'm a storyteller, a pretty nice feller. There's no need for you to be wary.
Get your act together, get light as a feather and fly down to the library.

We g-g-got . . . We g-g-got . . . We g-g-got . . . B-B-B-B-B-Books on . . .

Spiders saving pigs,
Boys eating worms,
Bunnies with fangs,
Scary books to make you squirm.

We got the Boxcar kids,
A curious monkey swinging by,
We have Ramona the Pest,
Hey! Sweet Valley High!

We have the knock-knock jokes,
Even old Doc Seuss.
You can draw a dinosaur
Or read Mama Goose.

We got records and tapes
And videocassettes.
Books 'bout Superfudge,
ABC's and BMX.

We know where sidewalks end
And where the wild things are.
We have Amelia Bedelia
And twinkle, twinkle, little star.

We have books to make you laugh,
Some to make you cry,
Nightmares in our closet,
Ladies swallowing flies.

We g-g-got books!

Now I've said my rap, think I'll take a nap.
Hope my dreams aren't scary.
'Cause when I wake up all new,
I'll find that my dreams have come true
'Cause I'm going to the library!

## "The New Rappin' Rob Rap (2002)"

By Rob Reid

(Insert these lines in the body of the original library rap)

Boys diggin' holes,
Boys swallowin' keys,
Chrysanthemum,
Minerva Louise.

A Winn-Dixie dog
And froggies that flew,
A princess diary and a
Click Clack Moo!

Olivia the pig,
The Redwall crew,
The Stinky Cheese Man
And others—PU!

We got your sideways stories
From a wayside school;
Or is it wayside stories
From a sideways school?

Yo! Yes? Chicka Boom
And a Zin! Zin! Zin!
A Lon Po Po,
I Spy! We win!

Hey! Junie B. Jones!
You know that we got her,
And how could we ever
Forget Harry Potter!

The next rap is a cross between a library scavenger hunt and an unscramble puzzle. The kids receive a copy of "The Messed-Up Rap" and listen to the rap performed. They work with partners to unscramble the book titles they know and use keyword searches on the online catalogue to decipher the rest. As a follow-up activity they could locate the books in the collection and write down the authors on their sheets. If your library doesn't contain all of the following books, write your own little messed-up rap.

## "The Messed-Up Rap"

### By Rob Reid

I'm Rappin' Rob and I'm confused,
I gotta puzzle with a lot of clues.
I read about 40 books last night
But I got 'em mixed up,

Somethin's not quite right.
I'm gonna ask ya please to help straighten 'em out,
'Cause I bet ya know books, without a doubt.
Listen carefully now and use your head,
Ready or not, here's what I read:

Thirteen Ways to Eat Fried Worms
Cloudy with a Chance of Caps for Sale
Millions of Very Hungry Caterpillars
Tales of a Fourth Grade Freckle Juice
The Day Jimmy's Boa Buzzed in People's Ears
Horton Hatches Blueberries for Sal
Island of the Blue Jumanji
The Little Engine That Could Wrinkle in Time
A Day No Pigs Would Make Way for Ducklings
From the Mixed-Up Files of Mr. Popper's Penguins
Animals Should Definitely Not Wear Corduroy
Brown Bear, Brown Bear, Where's Waldo?
If You Give a Mouse Stone Soup
The Sweet Valley Babysitters Club
Ramona, Plain and Tall
Free to Be . . . A Boy, a Dog, and a Frog
Nobody Asked Me If I Wanted a Nightmare in My Closet
The Lion, the Witch, and the Best Christmas Pageant Ever
Where the Red Fern, Wild Things, and the Sidewalk Ends
Green Eggs and the Terrible, Horrible, No Good, Very Bad Ham!

That's the Messed-Up Rap, now I'll take a break.
Please straighten these titles 'cause they give me an ache.
Then when you're done with that, I think it would be fun
If you took your two favorite books and messed them into one.
That's how you do the Messed-Up Rap,
You read a few books, put on your thinking cap.
Mix the words in a title and give a little snap,
Now you got your own little Messed-Up Rap.

*Key:*

1. *Thirteen Ways to Sink a Sub* by Jamie Gilson.
2. *How to Eat Fried Worms* by Thomas Rockwell.

3. *Cloudy with a Chance of Meatballs* by Judi Barrett.

4. *Caps for Sale* by Esphyr Slobodkina.

5. *Millions of Cats* by Wanda Gag.

6. *The Very Hungry Caterpillar* by Eric Carle.

7. *Tales of a Fourth Grade Nothing* by Judy Blume.

8. *Freckle Juice* by Judy Blume.

9. *The Day Jimmy's Boa Ate the Wash* by Trinka Hakes Noble.

10. *Why Mosquitoes Buzz in People's Ears* by Verna Aardema.

11. *Horton Hatches the Egg* by Dr. Seuss.

12. *Blueberries for Sal* by Robert McCloskey.

13. *Island of the Blue Dolphins* by Scott O'Dell.

14. *Jumanji* by Chris Van Allsburg.

15. *The Little Engine That Could* by Watty Piper.

16. *A Wrinkle in Time* by Madeleine L'Engle.

17. *A Day No Pigs Would Die* by Robert Newton Peck.

18. *Make Way for Ducklings* by Robert McCloskey.

19. *From the Mixed-Up Files of Mrs. Basil E. Frankweiler* by E. L. Konigsburg.

20. *Mr. Popper's Penguins* by Richard Atwater.

21. *Animals Should Definitely Not Wear Clothing* by Judi Barrett.

22. *Corduroy* by Don Freeman.

23. *Brown Bear, Brown Bear, What Do You See?* by Bill Martin Jr.

24. *Where's Waldo?* by Martin Handford.

25. *If You Give a Mouse a Cookie* by Laura Joffe Numeroff.

26. *Stone Soup* by Marcia Brown.

27. The Sweet Valley Twins series by Francine Pascal.

28. The Babysitters Club series by Ann Martin.

29. Ramona series by Beverly Cleary.

30. *Sarah, Plain and Tall* by Patricia McLachlan.

31. *Free to Be You and Me* by Marlo Thomas.

32. *A Boy, a Dog, and a Frog* by Mercer Mayer.

33. *Nobody Asked Me If I Wanted a Baby Sister* by Martha Alexander.

34. *There's a Nightmare in My Closet* by Mercer Mayer.

35. *The Lion, the Witch, and the Wardrobe* by C. S. Lewis.
36. *The Best Christmas Pageant Ever* by Barbara Robinson.
37. *Where the Red Fern Grows* by Wilson Rawls.
38. *Where the Wild Things Are* by Maurice Sendak.
39. *Where the Sidewalk Ends* by Shel Silverstein.
40. *Green Eggs and Ham* by Dr. Seuss.
41. *Alexander and the Terrible, Horrible, No Good, Very Bad Day* by Judith Viorst.

The next little ditty discusses one of the pet peeves in the library profession—pronouncing "library" as "li-berry."

### "The Li-Berry Rap"

#### By Rob Reid

Well, I'm Rappin' Rob and that's a fact!
I've come to get you and take you back.
Back on down to the li-*brary.*
And don't pronounce it li-*berry!*
We ain't a place for pickin' fruit.
So don't give me no raspberry toot.

Come check us out, this li-*brary,*
Just don't pronounce it li-*barey!*
This place won't break you, won't take your loot,
Come in your jeans, not your birthday suit.

I say-say slide on down to the li-*brary,*
Just don't pronounce it li-*beary!*
Corduroy's a bear and although he's real cute,
If you don't pronounce it right, I'm gonna give you the boot!

L-L-L-Li-*brary!*
L-L-L-Li-*brary!*
L-L-L-Li-*brary!*
Yeah, the Library!

Not the Li-*berry*,
Don't say the Li-*barey*,
It's not the Li-*beary*,
It's the Library!
Yeah!

## "The Read, Read, Read Chant"

By Rob Reid

*Chorus:*

Leader:　　Read, read, read, let's read.
Group:　　Read, read, read, let's read.
Leader:　　Read, read, read, let's read.
Group:　　Read, read, read, let's read.
Leader:　　Read in the kitchen, read in the park,
　　　　　Read in the day and read when it's dark.
　　　　　Read in the tub, read at school,
　　　　　Read in the fridge 'cause it's real cool.

　　　　　　　*(Chorus)*

Leader:　　Read to a dog, read to a cow,
　　　　　Read to a kitty cat and read to a sow,
　　　　　Read to your Barbie, read to your teddy,
　　　　　Read to your toys before you go to beddy.

　　　　　　　*(Chorus)*

Leader:　　Read at the gym while shooting hoops,
　　　　　Read at the restaurant while sipping soup,
　　　　　Read at the circus, read at the zoo,
　　　　　The monkeys are reading and so should you.

　　　　　　　*(Chorus)*

Leader:　　Read a mystery, guess the clue,
　　　　　Read something scary and then go "Boo!"
　　　　　Read at the pool, read in a tree,
　　　　　Read when you're alone and with your family.

　　　　　　　*(Chorus)*

　　　　　Read!

## "Traffic Light Activity"

### By Rob Reid

I use this activity to alert my audience that the program is ending. Make a simple felt traffic light out of one large rectangle and three circles: red, yellow, and green. Place it on your chest and say:

"I'm going to test you and see how well you can follow directions after sitting so long. Who knows what happens when you see a green light on the traffic light? Yes, it means go. I'm going to ask you to do a motion, like wave your hands. When you see the green light, wave them fast. When you see the yellow light, wave them slowly. When you see the red light, stop. I'm going to mix up the colors to see if you can follow along."

Cover up two of the colored circles. Move your hands quickly, exposing first the yellow light and then the red light. Then show only the green light to make the audience wave their hands quickly. As they do, say, "Ahhh, that feels good. It was getting hot up here. Just a little bit longer . . . and stop!"

Cover up the green and yellow circles and instruct the children to move their heads back and forth. Then show only the yellow circle, saying, "That's right, nice and slow."

Alternate showing the yellow and red circles again; then ask, "Are you having a good time?" To elicit the desired response, show only the green light, which will make the audience shake their heads up and down as if they were agreeing. To stop the nodding, show only the red circle.

Now vary the activity: "This time I'm going to ask you to clap your hands." Start out slowly by alternating between yellow and red circles. Then show only the green circle, which will cause great applause. Pretend to be astonished: "Why, thank you! I'm very touched. Thank you very much!"

If the audience stops clapping, point to the green circle. When they start up again, say, "Please! No more clapping!" As you protest, continue pointing to the green circle to encourage the applause, saying, "No, please stop. This is too much. I'm overcome with happiness. Bless you! I've never had a reception like this before."

Cover the green circle "accidentally," and look puzzled when the audience stops clapping. Then look down and discover that the red circle is exposed. Cover it sheepishly and show the green circle to get the applause going again. Then yank the felt traffic light off your chest, ask the audience to rise, and go into "Wave Goodbye."

## "Wave Goodbye"
By Rob Reid

Wave high,
    *(Wave high overhead)*
Wave low,
    *(Wave down by the ground)*
I think it's time,
We gotta go.
    *(Point to wrist)*

Wave your elbows,
    *(Wave elbows)*
Wave your toes,
    *(Wave feet)*
Wave your tongue,
    *(Wave tongue)*
And wave your nose.
    *(Wiggle nose)*

Wave your knees,
    *(Wave knees)*
Wave your lips,
    *(Move lips)*
Blow a kiss
With fingertips.
    *(Blow a kiss)*

Wave your ears,
    *(Wiggle ears)*
Wave your hair,
    *(Shake head)*
Wave your belly,
    *(Shake belly)*
And derrière.
    *(Shake hips)*

Wave your chin,
    *(Move chin)*

Wave your eye,
  *(Blink)*
Wave your hand,
  *(Wave hand)*
And say Goodbye!

Here's one more goodbye activity.

### "See Ya Later, Alligator"
#### Adapted by Rob Reid

See ya later, alligator.
After 'while, crocodile.
Hit the trail, cottontail.
Sayonara, piranha.
Outta sight, termite.
Start to jog, warthog.
Hit the road, horned toad.
To the park, aardvark.
Hang loose, gray goose.
Jump in the lake, rattlesnake.
Shake your rug, garden slug.
Put on your shoe, caribou.
Don't you whine, porcupine.
Start to squirm, earthworm.
Better flee, bumblebee.
Put on your hat, bobcat.
Say no more, condor.
Just go, hippo.

# 8

## The Funniest Books
## in Your Library

This section lists what I think are the funniest books in the library. I have used them extensively and have had great reactions from the kids. My lists are selective. There are many wonderful humor books that I didn't include. Please add your selections to my core lists. Entries are categorized as picture books, easy readers, juvenile fiction chapter books, poetry collections, and anthologies and folklore collections. The chapter ends with my personal Hall of Fame of the Funniest Children's Authors.

## PICTURE BOOKS

Aardema, Verna. *Who's in Rabbit's House?* Illustrated by Leo and Diane Dillon. Dial, 1977.

> Masai villagers don masks and tell the funny story of The Long One in Rabbit's house. The Long One threatens to eat trees and trample elephants. Frog offers to help, but Rabbit tells her to go away. Frog finally proves that The Long One is only a caterpillar. The illustration of the "real" lions on the last page is a scream.

Adler, David A. *Chanukah in Chelm.* Illustrated by Kevin O'Malley. Lothrop, 1997.

> Mendel helps the rabbi find a table for the menorah. He looks in the

closet. He moves a table to look for a table. He looks under the table. No table. He looks over the table. No table. The logic goes downhill from here while the humor quotient goes up. Humorous non-picture book collections of Chelm stories: Kimmel, Eric. *The Jar of Fools: Eight Hanukkah Stories from Chelm* (Holiday House, 2000); Singer, I. B. *Stories for Children* (Farrar, 1984).

Allard, Harry. *Miss Nelson Is Missing.* Illustrated by James Marshall. Houghton Mifflin, 1977.

The worst-behaved students in the whole school misbehaved enough to chase away their teacher, Miss Nelson. They soon shape up when confronted with the meanest substitute teacher in the world, Viola Swamp. Read Miss Nelson's lines in a quiet, timid voice and Viola Swamp's with a sharp tone. Sequels: *Miss Nelson Is Back* (Houghton Mifflin, 1982); *Miss Nelson Has a Field Day* (Houghton Mifflin, 1985).

Birdseye, Tom. *Soap! Soap! Don't Forget the Soap!* Illustrated by Andrew Glass. Holiday House, 1993.

Plug, who has a poor memory—"*no* one was as forgetful as Plug"—gets sent on an errand by his mother to buy some soap. On the way to the store he forgets that particular item and upsets several people. Since he has a bad habit of repeating the last phrase he hears, the folks he encounters think he is insulting them.

Bruchac, Joseph, and James Bruchac. *How Chipmunk Got His Stripes.* Illustrated by Jose Aruego and Ariane Dewey. Dial, 2001.

Little Brown Squirrel teases Bear once too often and acquires his stripes the hard way. Use contrasting voices for the two main characters. When Bear has Brown Squirrel under his paw, emphasize the line, "I cannot even breathe," through clenched teeth. When Bear and Brown Squirrel sit up all night, divide your audience in two with the first half chanting Bear's lines, "The sun will not come up, hummph," and the other half chanting Brown Squirrel's lines, "The sun is going to rise, oooh!"

Christelow, Eileen. *Five Little Monkeys Jumping on the Bed.* Clarion, 1989.

This picture book is based on the traditional and popular fingerplay. The fun illustrations show the monkeys getting their heads bandaged one by one. An increasingly frustrated doctor monkey says the key phrase, "No more monkeys jumping on the bed!" Once the five monkey children go to sleep, Mama starts jumping on her bed. Sequels: *Five Little Monkeys Sitting in a Tree* (Clarion, 1991); *Don't Wake Up Mama! Another Five Little Monkeys Story* (Clarion, 1992); *Five Little Monkeys with Nothing to Do* (Clarion, 1996); *Five Little Monkeys Wash the Car* (Clarion, 2000).

Cuyler, Margery. *That's Good! That's Bad!* Illustrated by David Catrow. Holt, 1991.

The author takes the traditional joke story game and uses it with a young boy who is separated from his family at the zoo. His parents give him a balloon. "Oh, that's good. No, that's bad!" The balloon carries him to the jungle. Sequel: *That's Good! That's Bad! In the Grand Canyon* (Holt, 2002).

DePaola, Tomie. *Fin M'Coul: The Giant of Knockmany Hill.* Holiday House, 1981.

Fin the giant is afraid of an even bigger giant, Cucullin. Fin's wife, Oonagh, saves the day by dressing Fin up as a baby and passing him off as his own son. Cucullin keeps losing his teeth and finally loses the brass finger that gives him his strength. Read Cucullin's lines in a gruff manner. The kids will enjoy spotting the sheep, the cat, and tiny men in the illustrations.

Dodds, Dayle Ann. *Sing, Sophie!* Illustrated by Rosanne Litzinger. Candlewick, 1997.

Sophie loves to sing at the top of her voice. Her singing is even louder than the thunderstorm that frightens Baby Jacob. "Yippee-ky-yee! Yippee-ky-yuu!" Sing Sophie's lines at the top of your voice. Melody is optional.

Ericsson, Jennifer A. *She Did It!* Illustrated by Nadine Bernard Westcott. Farrar, 2002.

Four sisters make messes throughout the house and yard. When their mother confronts them, they point to each other and yell, "She did it!" The audience will soon join in with this accusation. The ending is predictable, but satisfying.

Feiffer, Jules. *I Lost My Bear.* Morrow, 1998.

A young girl loses her teddy bear and drives her family crazy. Her sister instructs her to close her eyes and throw one of her other stuffed animals. "Sometimes it lands in the same place." The little girl's hysterics are fun to act out. Heavy on dialogue, this is especially good material for a reader's theater script.

Fleming, Candace. *Muncha! Muncha! Muncha!* Illustrated by G. Brian Karas. Atheneum, 2002.

Three rabbits "Tippy-Tippy-Tippy-Pat" into Mr. McGreeley's garden and munch on the produce. He builds bigger and bigger walls and deeper and deeper trenches, but the rabbits "Spring-Hurdle, Dash!" and "Dig-Scrabble, Scratch!" and "Dive-Paddle, Splash!" back to the garden. Their final trick is very clever.

Goble, Paul. *Iktomi and the Boulder.* Orchard, 1988.

Iktomi is a vain dandy who places his blanket on top of a boulder and then takes it back. The boulder chases Iktomi and pins him down. Several animals try to push the boulder off of him but fail. Finally, bats tear the boulder to bits. The humor lies in Iktomi's talent for getting into trouble. Sequels: *Iktomi and the Berries* (Orchard, 1989); *Iktomi and the Ducks* (Orchard, 1990); *Iktomi and the Buffalo Skull* (Orchard, 1991); *Iktomi and the Buzzard* (Orchard, 1994); *Iktomi and the Coyote* (Orchard, 1998); *Iktomi Loses His Eyes* (Orchard, 1999).

Hale, Lucretia. *The Lady Who Put Salt in Her Coffee.* Retold and illustrated by Amy Schwartz. Harcourt, 1989.

Instead of replacing mother's spoiled coffee with a new brew, the family consults experts who add all manner of chemicals and herbs in order to correct the taste. Adapted from *The Complete Peterkin Papers* (Houghton Mifflin, 1960).

Henkes, Kevin. *Julius, the Baby of the World.* Greenwillow, 1990.

Lilly is jealous of her new baby brother. When no one is looking, she insults him and mixes up the alphabet while he is sleeping in his crib. She also calls him "Julius, the Germ of the World." She just can't believe he's staying permanently. Because of her behavior, she spends more time than usual in the "uncooperative chair." Companion books: *Chester's Way* (Greenwillow, 1988); *Lilly's Purple Plastic Purse* (Greenwillow, 1998).

Hong, Lily Toy. *Two of Everything.* Whitman, 1993.

A magic pot duplicates everything placed inside of it. Mr. and Mrs. Haktak can't believe their good fortune. Mrs. Haktak then falls into the pot and two Mrs. Haktaks come out. Next we see two Mr. Haktaks. Afterward, the two sets of Haktaks become very good friends and neighbors. And they are very, very careful about what they put into the pot.

Kasza, Keiko. *Don't Laugh, Joe!* Putnam, 1997.

Joe, a possum, has a hard time learning the possum survival trick of playing dead. He keeps laughing because he's ticklish. While reading Joe's lines, laugh as if being tickled. Read the bear's lines in a low, slow voice.

Kellogg, Steven. *I Was Born About 10,000 Years Ago*. Morrow, 1996.

A group of kids one-up each other in the tall-tale department. They brag about everything from personally filling up the Sahara Desert with sand to playing hopscotch on the moon. This picture book is a perfect jumping-off point for a Liars' Club activity for older kids and enjoyable listening for the younger crowd.

Kellogg, Steven. *Sally Ann Thunder Ann Whirlwind Crockett*. Morrow, 1995.

At the age of one, Sally was the fastest runner in the state. She flipped the strongest arm wrestlers at four, and on her eighth birthday she set out to find adventure in the frontier. This tall tale will take care of itself. Simply read it in a bigger-than-life voice. Kellogg's other tall-tale picture books include: *Paul Bunyan* (Morrow, 1984); *Pecos Bill* (Morrow, 1986); *Johnny Appleseed* (Morrow, 1988); and *Mike Fink* (Morrow, 1992).

Kent, Jack. *The Caterpillar and the Polliwog*. Prentice-Hall, 1982.

An excited polliwog listens to a snotty caterpillar describe how she's going to turn into a beautiful butterfly. The polliwog assumes he'll turn into a butterfly, too. Pinch your nose to give the caterpillar's lines a snobbish tone.

Kent, Jack. *Little Peep*. Prentice-Hall, 1981.

The barnyard animals allow rooster to bully them because they believe that without his crowing the sun won't come up. A little chick tries crowing the sun up with his tiny voice. The kids will laugh as you read in your highest voice "Peep-a-deeple-peep!" and "Peep-a-doodle-peep!"

Ketteman, Helen. *Armadillo Tattletale*. Illustrated by Keith Graves. Scholastic, 2000.

Armadillo had large ears in the old days. He used them to eavesdrop on the other animals. He would mix up his gossip and pass on messages that caused hard feelings. The injured parties threw "hissy fits." Make faces and imitate the spluttery noises made during "hissy fits."

Kimmel, Eric. *Anansi and the Moss-Covered Rock.* Illustrated by Janet Stevens. Holiday House, 1988.

Anansi the spider finds a rock with mysterious powers. Saying the words "moss-covered rock" in its presence causes the speaker to faint. Anansi uses this power to trick the other animals and steal their food. The illustrations of the various animals lying prone are priceless. At the end of the story, repeat the title of the book and then pretend to faint (with a smile on your face). Sequels: *Anansi Goes Fishing* (Holiday House, 1992); *Anansi and the Talking Melon* (Holiday House, 1994); *Anansi and the Magic Stick* (Holiday House, 2001).

Lester, Helen. *Tacky the Penguin.* Illustrated by Lynn Munsinger. Houghton Mifflin, 1988.

Tacky is the odd penguin of the bunch. He wears a Hawaiian shirt, sings badly, makes cannonball dives, and marches out of step. His crazy antics scare away the mean hunters. Transform yourself into Tacky, complete with Hawaiian shirt: Sing badly, pretend to cannonball, and march out of step. Sequels: *Tacky in Trouble* (Houghton Mifflin, 1997); *Tacky and the Emperor* (Houghton Mifflin, 2000).

Lester, Julius. *Sam and the Tigers.* Illustrated by Jerry Pinkney. Dial, 1996.

Lester and Pinkney team up for a retelling of Little Black Sambo. In this version, the main character, Sam, and his parents, Sam and Sam, "live in a place called Sam-sam-sa-mara, where the animals and the people lived and worked together like they didn't know they weren't suppose to."

Lloyd, David. *Polly Molly Woof Woof: A Book About Being Happy.* Illustrated by Charlotte Hard. Candlewick, 2000.

Polly takes her dog Molly to the park where they meet more dogs. The audience is encouraged by the text to bark, sniff, and laugh out loud throughout the story.

London, Jonathan. *Froggy Gets Dressed.* Illustrated by Frank Remkiewicz. Viking, 1992.

This book is a lot of fun to read aloud with all of the sound effects London adds to the text. Froggy wakes up in the middle of winter and wants to play outside. His clothing makes "zoop," "zup," and "zwit" noises as he gets dressed. His mother constantly shouts "Frrrrooggyy!" Draw out this line long and loud. Froggy is embarrassed when he realizes he forgot his pants, coat, and underwear. Froggy appears in numerous sequels.

Lum, Kate. *What! Cried Granny: An Almost Bedtime Story*. Illustrated by Adrian Johnson. Dial, 1999.

Patrick spends the night at Granny's house, but there isn't a spare bed. "What?" cries Granny, who promptly chops down a tree, draws some plans, and builds and paints a new bed for Patrick. The scenario repeats itself when Granny learns Patrick also needs a pillow, blanket, and teddy bear. The audience will chime in and join you on your many, incredulous "What?!?s."

MacDonald, Alan. *Snarlyhissopus*. Illustrated by Louise Voce. Tiger Tales, 2002.

This is a picture book version of the telephone party game in which messages are whispered from one person to another and garbled along the way. Hippopotamus introduces himself to Pelican. Pelican, in turn, tells Monkey about the newcomer but describes Hippopotamus as "Spottyhippomus." As each animal tells another about the new creature, their fears grow. The names they pass on are fun to read aloud: "Woppabiggmouse," "Drippaslobbermouth," "Grippersnappertooth," "Gulpawobbletusk," and the title name.

MacDonald, Elizabeth. *The Wolf Is Coming!* Illustrated by Ken Brown. Dutton, 1997.

A wolf chases a family of rabbits and various barnyard creatures from one structure to another. The illustrations are hilarious—from the wide-eyed rabbits to the pig snouts and pig rears sticking out of a shack. Read the recurring phrase "The wolf is coming" in the vocal styles of the animal that says it (low for cow, shrill for pigs, etc.). Cue the audience to yell it with you at the end.

Massie, Diane Redfield. *The Baby Beebee Bird*. Illustrated by Steven Kellogg. HarperCollins, 2000.

The zoo animals can't sleep because of the Baby BeeBee Bird's nocturnal noises. Any book that has the reader say nearly 100 variations of

"Beebeebobbibobbi" is going to elicit laughs. Kellogg's meshing of text and original illustrations add to this updated version of a 1963 story.

Mathews, Judith, and Fay Robinson. *Nathaniel Willy, Scared Silly.* Illustrated by Alexi Natchev. Bradbury, 1994.

This version of the folktale "The Squeaky Door," with plenty of sound effects, is one of my favorites to read aloud. When the door goes "Eeeek!" make the sound at the top of your voice, loud enough to make the kids clap their hands over their ears. They will stare at you in disbelief for one second, then laugh at the thought of an adult being so noisy in the library. The illustrations of Grandma carrying the pig and the cow are hilarious.

McDermott, Gerald. *Zomo the Rabbit: A Trickster Tale from West Africa.* Harcourt, 1992.

Zomo is not content with being clever—he also wants wisdom. He gets it the hard way. Act out the movements of Big Fish dancing, Wild Cow charging, Leopard rolling (with your hands), and running in place for Zomo. Companion books: *Raven: A Trickster Tale from the Pacific Northwest* (Harcourt, 1993); *Coyote: A Trickster Tale from the American Southwest* (Harcourt, 1994); *Jabuti the Tortoise: A Trickster Tale from the Amazon* (Harcourt, 2001).

McFarland, Lyn Rossiter. *Widget.* Illustrated by Jim McFarland. Farrar, 2001.

Mrs. Diggs's cats, "the girls," don't like the new stray dog. However, he wins them over by meowing, puffing, hissing, spitting, and growling. When Mrs. Diggs passes out and the cats' growls don't attract anyone, Widget begins to bark. The cats join in with their own barks and help soon arrives. Great illustrations with "the girls" and Widget having a puffing standoff.

Meddaugh, Susan. *Martha Speaks.* Houghton Mifflin, 1992.

Martha the dog eats a bowl of alphabet soup. Instead of going to her stomach, the letters go to her brain and give her the ability to talk to her human family. Take the time to read the numerous dialogue balloons. "Mom says that fruitcake you sent wasn't fit for a dog. But I thought it was delicious." Sequels: *Martha Calling* (Houghton Mifflin, 1994); *Martha Blah Blah* (Houghton Mifflin, 1996); *Martha Walks the Dog* (Houghton Mifflin, 1998); *Martha and Skits* (Houghton Mifflin, 2000).

Miller, Sara Swan. *Three Stories You Can Read to Your Dog*. Illustrated by True Kelley. Houghton Mifflin, 1995.

These simple stories are told at a dog's level. Tell the dog about the time it heard a knock at the door and immediately thought "Burglar!" The reader has a chance to bark dozens of times. Or tell the dog about the time it dreamed about burying a bone and a bone tree grew. Companion books: *Three Stories You Can Read to Your Cat* (Houghton Mifflin, 1997); *Three More Stories You Can Read to Your Dog* (Houghton Mifflin, 2000); *Three More Stories You Can Read to Your Cat* (Houghton Mifflin, 2002).

Most, Bernard. *The Cow That Went Oink*. Harcourt, 1990.

A cow who can only oink meets a pig who can only moo. The other farm animals find this very amusing and laugh in their own styles: "Moo-Ha," "Oink-Ha," "Hee-Haw-Ha," "Cock-a-Doodle-Ha," and so on. The audience can chime in on the animal laughs. Cow and Pig, by the way, wisely ignore the other animals and practice their proper sounds: "Oimook," "Oinkoo," "Moink," and "Mook." They wind up bilingual, each able to "Moo" and "Oink."

Munsch, Robert. *Mortimer*. Illustrated by Michael Martchenko. Annick, 1985.

Mortimer's mother, father, seventeen brothers and sisters, and two policemen try to make him settle down and go to sleep with poor results. The audience will delight in singing Mortimer's song, "Clang, clang, rattle bing-bang, Gonna make my noise all day." They'll also join you in shouting "Mortimer, be quiet!"

Novak, Matt. *Mouse TV*. Orchard, 1994.

The tiny illustrations are hard to share with a large group and may be more humorous to parents. But they are funny. Tiny mice with facial hair and beehive hairdos, advertisements for Tres Squeak Fashions, and science shows featuring a mouse host listening to a panel of amphibians on the show "It's a Frog's Life" are just a small part of the fun.

Numeroff, Laura Joffe. *If You Give a Mouse a Cookie*. Illustrated by Felicia Bond. HarperCollins, 1985.

Sometimes I feel that this is the perfect picture book. The text makes a neat circle, and the illustrations make this the most expressive mouse in children's picture book-dom. Companion books: *If You Give a Moose a*

*Muffin* (HarperCollins, 1991); *If You Give a Pig a Pancake* (HarperCollins, 1998); *If You Take a Mouse to the Movies* (HarperCollins, 2000).

Pilkey, Dav. *Dog Breath: The Horrible Trouble with Hally Tosis.* Blue Sky, 1994.

A dog named Hally has breath powerful enough to scare skunks, cause grandmothers to faint, and make on-screen motion picture characters hold their noses. Hally saves the day when he licks two burglars, causing them to pass out cold.

Pinkwater, Daniel. *Author's Day.* Macmillan, 1993.

The Melvinville Elementary School invites Mr. Bramwell Wink-Porter, the author of *The Bunny Brothers,* for a school visit. However, everyone at the school mistakes Wink-Porter as the author of *The Fuzzy Bunny,* which was really written by Abigail Finkdotter. Pinkwater knows how to combine funny-sounding words with absurd situations to get laughs. All you have to do is read the lines.

Pinkwater, Daniel. *Tooth-Gnasher Superflash.* Macmillan, 1981.

The Popsnorkle family—just say the name Popsnorkle to get laughs— decides to trade in their old car, a green Thunderclap-Eight, and test-drive a Tooth-Gnasher Superflash. Enunciate the *p*'s on each Popsnorkle: "Mr. Popsnorkle and Mrs. Popsnorkle and the five little Popsnorkles." You can even make little snorting noises on *snorkle.*

Priceman, Marjorie. *How to Make an Apple Pie and See the World.* Knopf, 1994.

It's real easy to make an apple pie. However, if the market is closed, you may have to make a few side trips to places such as Europe, Sri Lanka, Jamaica, and Vermont to buy the ingredients.

Rathmann, Peggy. *Officer Buckle and Gloria.* Putnam, 1995.

Police dog Gloria helps perk up Officer Buckle's boring safety school assemblies. The fun comes from Gloria's antics behind the unknowing Officer Buckle's back. Share the many safety tips on the endpapers, such as "never put anything in your nose," which shows Gloria with a banana in her nose.

Root, Phyllis. *One Duck Stuck.* Illustrated by Jane Chapman. Candlewick, 1998.

Duck gets stuck in this counting book. Two fish, three moose, four crickets, five frogs, six skunks, seven snails, eight possums, nine snakes, and ten dragonflies rally to help. Be sure to exaggerate Root's liberal use of assonance: "The duck stays stuck in the muck down by the soggy, loggy marsh."

Ross, Tony. *Mrs. Goat and Her Seven Little Kids.* Atheneum, 1990.

Wolf's voice is deep and gruff when he first knocks on the door of the goat family. Then he tries to imitate Big Mother Goat's "squeaky little voice." Do the same.

Roth, Susan. *It's a Dog's New York.* National Geographic, 2001.

A New York City dog, who speaks a canine brand of New York–ese, tells newcomer Pepper all about the big city: "Ask me howda get to Cawnagee Hoall! . . . Ya hafta practice!"

Sadler, Marilyn. *Alistair in Outer Space.* Illustrated by Roger Bollen. Simon & Schuster, 1984.

Alistair is a very neat and punctual young man. He even puts his shoes in plastic bags at night. When a spaceship picks him up and leads him to several adventures with Goots and Trollabobbles, does he get excited? No, he simply worries about returning his library books on time. A perfect book for a library setting. Assure your story hour kids that if they get whisked away by a spaceship, they won't have to worry about their library books. Sequels: *Alistair's Elephant* (Simon & Schuster, 1983); *Alistair's Time Machine* (Simon & Schuster, 1984); *Alistair Underwater* (Simon & Schuster, 1990); *Alistair and the Alien Invasion* (Simon & Schuster, 1994).

Schneider, Howie. *Chewy Louie.* Rising Moon, 2000.

The new puppy chews everything—starting with the dogfood dish and soon the house itself. When the family believes the dog has finally outgrown his nasty habit, the reader comes to the final page, complete with a bite taken out of the corner.

Seuss, Dr. *Horton Hatches the Egg.* Random, 1940.

Mayzie, the lazy bird, asks Horton, the elephant, to sit on her egg. Some hunters, amazed at the sight of an elephant in a tree, sell Horton to the circus. Horton sticks with the egg in the nest because "an elephant's faithful—one hundred per cent."

Seuss, Dr. *The Sneetches and Other Stories.* Random, 1961.

> We meet Star-Belly Sneetches, who think they're better than the Plain-Belly Sneetches; the North-Going Zax who confronts the equally stubborn South-Going Zax; and the "pants with nobody inside 'em." Impress your audience by memorizing "Too Many Daves."

Seuss, Dr. *Yertle the Turtle and Other Stories.* Random, 1950.

> In addition to the story of the power-hungry turtle, Dr. Seuss gives us Gertrude McFuzz, the bird with the short, plain tail; and "The Big Brag," a story that features a rabbit who claims to hear a fly cough ninety miles away. He is upstaged by a bear who claims to smell a stale egg over six hundred miles away, and a worm who claims to be able to see around the world.

Shannon, David. *Duck on a Bike.* Blue Sky, 2002.

> When Duck rides a child's bike around the farm, the other animals scoff at him. But when several kids arrive at the farm and leave their bikes outside, the other farm animals get big grins on their faces. This particular illustration is a hoot.

Shannon, David. *No, David!* Blue Sky, 1998.

> Hilarious, two-page spreads of David getting into trouble make this a fun book to share. Naughty David is captured with his finger up his nostril, running down the street in his birthday suit, and chewing with his mouth wide open (although, if you look carefully, you'll see that he's eating a very nutritious meal). Sequel: *David Goes to School* (Blue Sky, 1999).

Shaw, Nancy. *Sheep in a Jeep.* Illustrated by Margot Apple. Houghton Mifflin, 1986.

> Shaw and her sheep can get more laughs from expressive illustrations and few words than almost anyone else in the business. Her books are so much fun to read aloud. Read slowly and savor the alliteration and assonance. The sheep crash their jeep in this volume. Sequels: *Sheep in a Shop* (Houghton Mifflin, 1991); *Sheep Out to Eat* (Houghton Mifflin, 1992); *Sheep Take a Hike* (Houghton Mifflin, 1994); *Sheep Trick or Treat* (Houghton Mifflin, 1997).

Sierra, Judy. *Counting Crocodiles.* Illustrated by Will Hillenbrand. Harcourt, 1997.

> A monkey, tired of eating lemons, counts several crocodiles who reside

in the Sillabobble Sea to reach an island with bananas. Kids will giggle at the sight of crocodiles in pink mohawks and "dressed like Goldilocks."

Sloat, Teri. *The Thing That Bothered Farmer Brown*. Illustrated by Nadine Bernard Westcott. Orchard, 1995.

Farmer Brown is bothered by a pesky mosquito. His swatting disturbs the farm animals. Swat the table hard to make your audience jump. Don't do this if there are very young children in the audience. Again, I speak from experience. The audience can help make the mosquito's "tiny, whiny, humming sound." Sequels: *Farmer Brown Goes Round and Round* (Dorling Kindersley, 1999); *Farmer Brown Shears His Sheep* (Dorling Kindersley, 2000).

Small, David. *Imogene's Antlers*. Crown, 1985.

"On Thursday, Imogene woke up, and found she had grown antlers." Imogene discovers both how hard it is to have antlers on her head and also how helpful. "You'll be lots of fun to decorate come Christmas." Her mother faints repeatedly with a thud!

Stanley, Diane. *Saving Sweetness*. Illustrated by G. Brian Karas. Putnam, 1996.

A sheriff sets off to rescue a runaway orphan but winds up getting rescued time and time again by her. Read the narrative as a grizzly, old western movie character.

Steig, William. *Doctor De Soto*. Farrar, 1982.

The famous mouse dentist cleverly treats a fox to avoid being eaten. After treating the fox's bad tooth, Doctor De Soto temporarily glues its jaws shut. The fox can't do anything but mutter, "Frank oo berry mush."

Steig, William. *Pete's a Pizza*. HarperCollins, 1998.

Pete is bored, so his parents pretend to turn him into a pizza. They apply oil (water), flour (talcum powder), tomatoes (checkers), and cheese (pieces of paper). He warns them that "pizza makers are not supposed to tickle their pizzas."

Stevens, Janet. *Coyote Steals the Blanket*. Holiday House, 1993.

Coyote steals a blanket from a rock that chases him in a threatening way. The humor lies in the illustrations, especially the images of the mule deer and bighorn sheep when they encounter the rock.

Stevens, Janet. *Tops and Bottoms*. Harcourt, 1995.

Rabbit and his family trick a very lazy bear out of the best crops. Stevens cleverly designed her book in a vertical, two-page spread format. Read bear's lines, "Uh, let's see. I'll take the top half, Hare," in a low, drowsy voice in contrast to Rabbit's brisk, energetic delivery—"It's a done deal, Bear."

Stevenson, James. *Could Be Worse!* Greenwillow, 1977.

This is the first in a long line of picture books with Grandpa telling tall tales of his childhood to his grandchildren. Grandpa's memory of himself shows him sporting a mustache as a child. There are over a dozen fun sequels featuring Grandpa.

Stevenson, James. *Don't Make Me Laugh*. Farrar, 1999.

Mr. Frimdimpny, an alligator, and other characters implore the reader to not laugh or smile at any of the goings-on in the book. Take a lesson from Stevenson and ask your audience not to laugh at any time during the story program.

Stevenson, James. *Worse than the Worst*. Greenwillow, 1994.

The worst person in the world meets his match in his great-nephew Warren. When the worst person in the world tries to make a collect call to Warren's parents to prevent his visit, they refuse to accept his call. "Tell them it's their uncle," he says. "They know that," the operator replies. Sequels: *The Worst Person in the World* (Greenwillow, 1978); *The Worst Person in the World at Crab Beach* (Greenwillow, 1988); *The Worst Person's Christmas* (Greenwillow, 1991); *The Worst Person Goes South* (Greenwillow, 1995).

Stoeke, Janet Morgan. *Minerva Louise*. Dutton, 1988.

Minerva Louise is a chicken who explores a house and decides that the fireplace is a perfect nest, a flowerpot is a comfortable chair, and the cat is a cow. Sequels: *A Hat for Minerva Louise* (Dutton, 1994); *Minerva Louise at School* (Dutton, 1996); *A Friend for Minerva Louise* (Dutton, 1997); *Minerva Louise at the Fair* (Dutton, 2000).

Van Laan, Nancy. *The Tiny, Tiny Boy and the Big, Big Cow*. Illustrated by Marjorie Priceman. Knopf, 1993.

A tiny, tiny boy wants to milk the big, big cow, but she won't stand still. The boy runs off crying to his mother for advice. Read the boy's lines in a whiny voice. A funnier version (but long out of print) is Marcia Sewall's *The Wee, Wee Mannie and the Big, Big Coo: A Scottish Folk Tale* (Little, Brown, 1977).

Vaughan, Marcia K. *Wombat Stew.* Illustrated by Pamela Lofts. Silver Burdett, 1984.

A dingo catches a wombat and sings, "Wombat stew / Wombat stew / Gooey, brewy / Yummy, chewy / Wombat stew!" Wombat is saved by his friends Platypus, Emu, Old Blue Tongue the Lizard, Echidna, and Koala. I interrupt the story by asking, "Do you know what an echidna is? Well, it's a small, tiny . . . oh, go ask a librarian!" I repeat variations of this line for the other Australian animals.

Viorst, Judith. *Alexander and the Terrible, Horrible, No Good, Very Bad Day.* Illustrated by Ray Cruz. Atheneum, 1972.

The things that ruin Alexander's day include waking up with gum in his hair, having a cavity, buying plain old white sneakers, and having lima beans for supper. Kids will chime in with the long title refrain. You, as the reader, will be a hit if you read Alexander's narrative as if you yourself were having a bad day. Sequels: *Alexander, Who Used to Be Rich Last Sunday* (Atheneum, 1978); *Alexander, Who's Not (Do You Hear Me? I Mean It!) Going to Move* (Atheneum, 1995).

Waber, Bernard. *Bearsie Bear and the Surprise Sleepover Party.* Houghton Mifflin, 1997.

Practice reading this rollicking book several times. Dazzle your audience with a tongue-twisting rendition of the cumulative story. Several animals beg Bearsie Bear to let them sleep in his cabin one cold winter's night. "It's me, Moosie Moose," said Moosie Moose. "Moosie Moose?" said Bearsie Bear. "Yes, Moosie Moose," said Moosie Moose. An especially good choice for a reader's theater script.

Waber, Bernard. *Ira Sleeps Over.* Houghton Mifflin, 1972.

Ira frets about taking his teddy bear to a sleepover. He's afraid that his friend will laugh and think Ira is a baby. Instead of reassuring her brother, Ira's sister torments him. "'He won't laugh,' said my mother. 'He won't laugh,' said my father. 'He'll laugh,' said my sister." Have fun playing around with the wonderful dialogue. Sequel: *Ira Says Goodbye* (Houghton Mifflin, 1988).

Wells, Rosemary. *Bunny Money.* Dial, 1997.

> Max and Ruby go on a shopping trip for their grandmother's birthday present. She winds up getting gifts that every grandmother cherishes— plastic glow-in-the-dark vampire teeth and musical bluebird earrings. Max buys himself plastic vampire teeth "with oozing cherry syrup inside." Wells encourages readers to photocopy the bunny money on the endpapers. They make a great library story program souvenir. Max and Ruby appear in several companion books.

Wiesner, David. *Tuesday.* Clarion, 1991.

> This nearly wordless book has stunning images of frogs flying on lily pads throughout the night. Let children linger over the pictures and spot the funny details, such as the frog waving through the window and another frog manipulating a television remote with its tongue.

Wood, Audrey. *The Bunyans.* Illustrated by David Shannon. Scholastic, 1996.

> Meet Paul, his wife, and two children. All are responsible for the creation of Mammoth Cave, Niagara Falls, Bryce Canyon, the Great Sand Dunes of Colorado, Big Sur, the Continental Divide, Old Faithful, and more.

Yorinks, Arthur. *Company's Coming.* Illustrated by David Small. Crown, 1988.

> What would you do if a spaceship with little aliens landed in your yard? Would you let them use the bathroom? Invite them for dinner? If you did, as Shirley and Moe did in this book, you might receive a lovely blender from the aliens in return for your hospitality. Sequel: *Company's Going* (Hyperion, 2001).

## Fractured Fairy Tales

Fractured fairy tales—a form of derivative literature—are inherently funny. The majority of these titles are in picture book format and many would appear side by side with the funniest picture books ever written.

### AESOP'S FABLES

Dinardo, Jeffrey. *The Wolf Who Cried Boy.* Grosset, 1989.

> The wolf is the one playing tricks on his neighbors.

Hartman, Bob. *The Wolf Who Cried Boy.* Illustrated by Tim Raglin. Putnam, 2002.

Little Wolf, tired of Lamburgers and Sloppy Does, cries "Boy" to get his way. In the end, a troop of Boy Scouts appears.

Kraus, Robert. *Fables Aesop Never Wrote.* Viking, 1994.

New versions include "The Wolf Who Cried 'Boy'" and "The City Moose and the Country Moose."

Levine, Gail Carson. *Betsy Who Cried Wolf.* Illustrated by Scott Nash. HarperCollins, 2000.

Betsy sets out to be the best shepherd ever.

Rosenthal, Paul. *Yo, Aesop! Get a Load of These Fables!* Illustrated by Marc Rosenthal. Simon & Schuster, 1998.

Nine updated fables with a silly commentary by Aesop himself.

Scieszka, Jon. *Squids Will Be Squids: Fresh Morals, Beastly Fables.* Illustrated by Lane Smith. Viking, 1998.

New fables, new characters, and new morals, such as "There are plenty of things to say to a hopping mad grasshopper mom. 'I don't know' is not one of them."

## CHICKEN LITTLE/HENNY PENNY

Palatini, Margie. *Earthquack!* Illustrated by Barry Moser. Simon & Schuster, 2002.

Little Chucky Ducky is alarmed. "'The earth is crumbling! The earth is crumbling! It's a quake,' quacked the duck."

## CINDERELLA

Buehner, Caralyn. *Fanny's Dream.* Illustrated by Mark Buehner. Dial, 1996.

Fanny Agnes has a Cinderella-type wish.

Climo, Shirley. *The Irish Cinderlad.* Illustrated by Loretta Krupinski. HarperCollins, 1996.

Big-footed Becan saves a princess and leaves behind one of his big boots, which is used to identify him.

Cole, Babette. *Prince Cinders.* Putnam, 1988.

    Cinders has a chance to go to the disco.

Compton, Joanne. *Ashpet: An Appalachian Tale.* Illustrated by Kenn Compton. Holiday House, 1994.

    Old Granny helps Ashpet go to the church picnic.

Edwards, Pamela Duncan. *Dinorella: A Prehistoric Fairy Tale.* Illustrated by Henry Cole. Hyperion, 1997.

    A Fairydactyl helps a dinosaur attend the Dinosaur Dance.

Holub, Joan. *Cinderdog and the Wicked Stepcat.* Whitman, 2001.

    Dogs and cats act out the Cinderella story at the Gitalong Ranch.

Jackson, Ellen. *Cinder Edna.* Illustrated by Kevin O'Malley. Lothrop, 1994.

    Lively Cinder Edna lives next door to the dull Cinderella.

Johnston, Tony. *Bigfoot Cinderrrrella.* Illustrated by James Warhola. Putnam, 1998.

    Bigfoot Prince is helped by a beary godfather.

Ketteman, Helen. *Bubba the Cowboy Prince: A Fractured Texas Tale.* Illustrated by James Warhola. Scholastic, 1997.

    Cinderella is a cowboy and the fairy godmother is a cow.

Lattimore, Deborah Nourse. *Cinderhazel: The Cinderella of Halloween.* Scholastic, 1997.

    And they all lived "filthily ever after."

Lowell, Susan. *Cindy Ellen: A Wild Western Cinderella.* Illustrated by Jane Manning. HarperCollins, 2000.

    Yet another version set in the western United States. This time Cindy Ellen loses her diamond spur.

Meddaugh, Susan. *Cinderella's Rat.* Houghton Mifflin, 1997.

    One of the rats who turned into a coachman tells his version of the story.

Minters, Frances. *Cinder-Elly.* Illustrated by G. Brian Karas. Viking, 1994.

    Cinderella loses her glass sneaker in this rap version.

Myers, Bernice. *Sidney Rella and the Glass Sneaker.* Macmillan, 1985.
Sidney becomes a football player thanks to the fairy godmother.

Perlman, Janet. *Cinderella Penguin, or, The Glass Flipper.* Viking, 1992.
Cinderella waddles to the ball.

San Souci, Robert D. *Cinderella Skeleton.* Illustrated by David Catrow. Silver Whistle, 2000.
Cinderella loses her whole foot.

Schroeder, Alan. *Smoky Mountain Rose: An Appalachian Cinderella.* Illustrated by Brad Sneed. Dial, 1997.
Cinderella goes square dancing with the aid of a fairy godmother hog.

Thaler, Mike. *Cinderella Bigfoot.* Illustrated by Jared Lee. Cartwheel, 1997.
Cinderella's feet are *really* big.

Yorinks, Arthur. *Ugh.* Illustrated by Richard Egielski. Farrar, 1990.
Cinderella is a cave boy named Ugh.

## THE EMPEROR'S NEW CLOTHES

Anholt, Laurence. *The Emperor's New Underwear.* Illustrated by Arthur Robbins. Meadowbrook, 1999.
Folks comment about the invisible underwear.

Calmenson, Stephanie. *The Principal's New Clothes.* Illustrated by Denise Brunkus. Scholastic, 1989.
Principal Bundy is tricked into appearing at a school assembly clad only in his underwear.

DeLuise, Dom. *King Bob's New Clothes.* Illustrated by Christopher Santoro. Simon & Schuster, 1996.
King Discombobulated stars in this retelling.

Goode, Diane. *The Dinosaur's New Clothes.* Blue Sky, 1999.
The emperor is a tyrannosaurus rex.

Lasky, Kathryn. *The Emperor's Old Clothes.* Illustrated by David Catrow. Harcourt, 1999.

A farmer finds the emperor's discarded finery and wears them as he does his chores.

Perlman, Janet. *The Emperor Penguin's New Clothes*. Viking, 1995.

The characters are the same penguins that populate the book *Cinderella Penguin.*

Yolen, Jane. *King Long Shanks*. Illustrated by Victoria Chess. Harcourt, 1998.

The frog king looks "toadally majestic" and "ribeting" in his new clothes.

## THE FROG PRINCE

Calmenson, Stephanie. *The Frog Principal*. Illustrated by Denise Brunkus. Scholastic, 2001.

The principal from *The Principal's New Clothes* gets changed into a frog by an incompetent magician.

Gwynne, Fred. *Pondlarker.* Simon & Schuster, 1990.

A frog goes looking for a kiss from a princess.

Hopkins, Jackie. *The Horned Toad Prince*. Illustrated by Michael Austin. Peachtree, 2000.

A cowgirl makes a deal with a horned toad.

Scieszka, Jon. *The Frog Prince Continued*. Illustrated by Steve Johnson. Viking, 1991.

The prince looks for a witch who can turn him back into a frog.

## THE GINGERBREAD MAN

Egielski, Richard. *The Gingerbread Boy.* HarperCollins, 1997.

This urban version has the main character chased by a rat and subway musicians.

Kimmel, Eric. *The Runaway Tortilla*. Illustrated by Randy Cecil. Winslow, 2000.

The tortilla encounters Señor Coyote in Texas.

## GOLDILOCKS AND THE THREE BEARS

Denim, Sue. *The Dumb Bunnies*. Illustrated by Dav Pilkey. Scholastic, 1994.

This bunny version of Goldilocks features a not-too-bright cast of characters set in the *Goodnight Moon* room.

Ernst, Lisa Campbell. *Goldilocks Returns*. Simon & Schuster, 2000.

Goldilocks shows up thirty years later with a guilty conscience.

Fearnley, Jan. *Mr. Wolf and the Three Bears*. Harcourt, 2002.

Goldilocks crashes yet another party.

Granowsky, Alvin. *Bears Should Share!* Illustrated by Annie Lunsford. Steck-Vaughn, 1996.

Goldilocks claims that Little Bear gave her permission to enter the bears' house while they were gone.

Guarnaccia, Steven. *Goldilocks and the Three Bears: A Tale Moderne*. Abrams, 2000.

These bears are very hip.

Lowell, Susan. *Dusty Locks and the Three Bears*. Illustrated by Randy Cecil. Holt, 2001.

Dusty sneaks into the cabin of the grizzlies.

MacDonald, Alan. *Beware of the Bears*. Illustrated by Gwyneth Williamson. Little Tiger, 1998.

The bears retaliate by trashing what they think is Goldilocks's house.

Marshall, James. *Goldilocks and the Three Bears*. Dial, 1988.

Not a true fractured tale, but it's hard to find a funnier retelling of this classic story.

May, Paul. *You're a Big Bear Now, Winston Brown*. Illustrated by Selina Young. Dorling Kindersley, 2001.

Winston proves he's big and brave when faced with an intruder.

Petach, Heidi. *Goldilocks and the Three Hares*. Putnam, 1995.

Goldilocks falls into the hares' hole, eats their oatmeal, and feels queasy on their waterbed.

Rosales, Melodye. *Leola and the Honeybears.* Cartwheel, 1999.

> An African American retelling of Goldilocks and the Three Bears. Leola encounters a weasel in the woods.

Tolhurst, Marilyn. *Somebody and the Three Blairs.* Illustrated by Simone Abel. Orchard, 1991.

> A bear explores the home of the Blair family.

Turkle, Brinton. *Deep in the Forest.* Dutton, 1976.

> A curious bear explores a cabin in the forest.

## HANSEL AND GRETEL

Thaler, Mike. *Hanzel and Pretzel.* Illustrated by Jared Lee. Cartwheel, 1997.

> The kids outwit and outeat the witch.

## JACK AND THE BEANSTALK

Anholt, Laurence. *Silly Jack and the Beanstalk.* Illustrated by Arthur Robbins. Simon & Schuster, 1999.

> Jack climbs a stack of baked bean tins.

Birdseye, Tom. *Look Out, Jack! The Giant Is Back.* Illustrated by Will Hillenbrand. Holiday House, 2001.

> The giant's brother is after Jack and his mom.

Briggs, Raymond. *Jim and the Beanstalk.* Coward, 1970.

> Jim meets the son of the original giant.

Harris, Jim. *Jack and the Giant: A Story Full of Beans.* Rising Moon, 1997.

> A cowboy version with a cattle-rustlin' giant.

Holub, Joan. *Jack and the Jellybeanstalk.* Illustrated by Benton Mahan. Grosset, 2002.

> A rabbit climbs up a beanstalk full of jellybeans.

Osborne, Mary Pope. *Kate and the Beanstalk.* Illustrated by Giselle Potter. Atheneum, 2000.

> A female protagonist climbs the beanstalk.

## THE LITTLE RED HEN

Oppenheim, Joanne. *"Not Now!" Said the Cow.* Illustrated by Chris Demarest. Gareth Stevens, 1997.

Little Black Crow plays the role of the Little Red Hen.

Stevens, Janet, and Susan Stevens Crummel. *Cook-A-Doodle-Doo.* Harcourt, 1999.

Big Brown Rooster, the great-grandson of Little Red Hen, sets out to bake a strawberry shortcake.

Sturges, Philemon. *The Little Red Hen (Makes a Pizza).* Illustrated by Amy Walrod. Dutton, 1999.

No one will help the hen make a pizza. She constantly runs to buy the ingredients "and some other stuff."

## LITTLE RED RIDING HOOD

Artell, Mike. *Petite Rouge: A Cajun Red Riding Hood.* Illustrated by Jim Harris. Dial, 2001.

A young duck, on her way to Grandmere's house, runs into Claude, an alligator.

Emberley, Michael. *Ruby.* Little, Brown, 1990.

Ruby the mouse outwits a cat on the way to Granny's house.

Ernst, Lisa Campbell. *Little Red Riding Hood: A Newfangled Prairie Tale.* Simon & Schuster, 1995.

The Grandma in this story turns out to be the original Little Red Riding Hood.

Lowell, Susan. *Little Red Cowboy Hat.* Illustrated by Randy Cecil. Holt, 1997.

Little Red delivers a jar of cactus jelly in this Southwest United States version.

Porter, Sue. *Little Wolf and the Giant.* Simon & Schuster, 1990.

Little Wolf encounters a giant on the way to Granny's house.

## MOTHER GOOSE NURSERY RHYMES

Aylesworth, Jim. *The Completed Hickory Dickory Dock.* Illustrated by Eileen Christelow. Atheneum, 1990.

We learn what happened when the clock struck two (and three, four, up through twelve).

Babcock, Chris. *No Moon, No Milk*. Illustrated by Mark Teague. Crown, 1993.

The great-great-granddaughter of the cow who jumped over the moon wants her turn.

Choldenko, Gennifer. *Moonstruck: The True Story of the Cow Who Jumped Over the Moon*. Illustrated by Paul Yalowitz. Hyperion, 1997.

A horse describes the events leading up to the historic moon jump.

Jackson, Alison. *If the Shoe Fits*. Illustrated by Karla Firehammer. Holt, 2001.

The old lady who lived in the shoe looks for new living quarters and runs into several nursery rhyme characters.

Kent, Jack. *Mrs. Mooley*. Artists and Writers Guild, 1993.

A cow is inspired by the nursery rhyme to jump over the moon.

Lansky, Bruce. *The New Adventures of Mother Goose*. Illustrated by Stephen Carpenter. Meadowbrook, 1993.

Highlights include Jack burning his pants jumping over the candlestick and Old Mother Hubbard's dog ordering pizza when the cupboard was bare.

Martin, David. *Five Little Piggies*. Illustrated by Susan Meddaugh. Candlewick, 1998.

The littlest piggie goes "Wee wee wee" all the way home because she has to go "wee wee."

Miranda, Anne. *To Market, to Market*. Illustrated by Janet Stevens. Harcourt, 1997.

Chaos reigns during this shopping trip.

O'Malley, Kevin. *Humpty Dumpty Egg-Splodes*. Walker, 2001.

Humpty goes berserk in Mother Goose Land while Mother Goose is away.

Palatini, Margie. *The Web Files*. Illustrated by Richard Egielski. Hyperion, 2001.

Ductective Web solves the case of the missing peppers in this *Dragnet/* gangster movie parody featuring several nursery rhyme characters.

Scieszka, Jon. *The Book That Jack Wrote.* Illustrated by Daniel Adel. Viking, 1994.

Several literary characters cause a chain reaction that results in the book falling on Jack.

Stevens, Janet, and Susan Stevens Crummel. *And the Dish Ran Away with the Spoon.* Harcourt, 2001.

Cat, Cow, and Dog look for the runaway Dish and Spoon.

Vail, Rachel. *Over the Moon.* Illustrated by Scott Nash. Orchard, 1998.

The cow keeps forgetting to jump over the moon during rehearsals. Instead, she jumps under, next to, and through the moon.

## THE PRINCESS AND THE PEA

Auch, Mary Jane. *The Princess and the Pizza.* Illustrated by Herm Auch. Holiday House, 2002.

This princess knows better than to fall for the old pea-under-the-mattress trick.

Johnston, Tony. *The Cowboy and the Black-Eyed Pea.* Illustrated by Warren Ludwig. Putnam, 1992.

A young woman places a pea under the saddles of her suitors to see who is the most sensitive.

Levine, Gail Carson. *The Princess Test.* HarperCollins, 1999.

This chapter book describes how sickly Lorelei somehow passes the awesome tests that King Humphrey and Queen Hermione have set up for their son's suitors.

Vaes, Alain. *The Princess and the Pea.* Little, Brown, 2001.

This princess is a mechanic in overalls.

## RAPUNZEL

Vozar, David. *RAPunzel: A Happenin' Rap.* Illustrated by Betsy Lewin. Doubleday, 1998.

This hip version features dog characters.

## RUMPELSTILTSKIN

Stanley, Diane. *Rumpelstiltskin's Daughter.* Morrow, 1997.

> Rumpelstiltskin married the miller's daughter, and this is their daughter's story.

## THE SHOEMAKER AND THE ELVES

Lowell, Susan. *The Bootmaker and the Elves.* Illustrated by Tom Curry. Orchard, 1997.

> The boot maker is so poor that even his shadow has holes in it. The story is set in the Old West.

## SLEEPING BEAUTY

Minters, Frances. *Sleepless Beauty.* Illustrated by G. Brian Karas. Viking, 1996.

> Beauty falls under a spell after touching a phonograph needle.

Yolen, Jane. *Sleeping Ugly.* Illustrated by Diane Stanley. Coward, 1981.

> Princess Miserella and Plain Jane fall under a sleeping spell.

## THE THREE BILLY GOATS GRUFF

Emberley, Rebecca. *Three Cool Kids.* Little, Brown, 1995.

> Inner-city setting with a rat in the role of the troll.

Hopkins, Jackie Mims. *The Three Armadillies Tuff.* Illustrated by S. G. Brooks. Peachtree, 2002.

> Three armadillos try to get past a mean old coyote who's blocking a culvert under the highway.

## THE THREE LITTLE PIGS

Allen, Jonathan. *Who's at the Door.* Morrow, 1993.

> The wolf tries on various disguises to get in.

Asch, Frank. *Ziggy Piggy and the Three Little Pigs.* Kids Can Press, 1998.

> The fourth little pig heads for the beach while the others build houses.

Celsi, Teresa Noel. *The Fourth Little Pig*. Illustrated by Doug Cushman. Raintree, 1990.

The sister of the three pigs helps them overcome their fears.

Cresp, Gael. *The Tale of Gilbert Alexander Pig*. Illustrated by David Cox. Barefoot Books, 2000.

A wolf follows Gilbert, knocking down his shelters and trying to steal his trumpet.

Harris, Jim. *The Three Little Dinosaurs*. Pelican, 1999.

The wolf character is played by a tyrannosaurus.

Hooks, William H. *The Three Little Pigs and the Fox*. Illustrated by S. D. Schindler. Macmillan, 1989.

Hamlet saves her brothers Rooter and Honker from a fox.

Laverde, Arlene. *Alaska's Three Pigs*. Illustrated by Mindy Dwyer. Sasquatch, 2000.

The wolf's role is played by a grizzly.

Lowell, Susan. *The Three Little Javelinas*. Illustrated by Jim Harris. Northland, 1992.

The pigs make their houses out of tumbleweed, saguaro ribs, and adobe bricks. Coyote is the bad guy.

McNaughton, Colin. *Yum!* Harcourt, 1999.

The pig tries to convince the wolf to get a job.

Scieszka, Jon. *The True Story of the Three Little Pigs*. Illustrated by Lane Smith. Viking, 1989.

This book is easily the most popular fractured fairy tale today. The wolf tells his side of the story.

Trivizas, Eugene. *The Three Little Wolves and the Big Bad Pig*. Illustrated by Helen Oxenbury. Margaret K. McElderry, 1993.

This is my personal favorite fractured fairy tale. Three fluffy, gentle wolves are threatened by one huge pig.

Walton, Rick. *Pig, Pigger, Piggest*. Illustrated by Jimmy Holder. Gibbs Smith, 1997.

Witches blow down the pigs' castles.

Whatley, Bruce. *Wait! No Paint!* HarperCollins, 2001.

> The pigs are in jeopardy from the wolf because the illustrator ran out of art supplies.

Wiesner, David. *The Three Pigs.* Clarion, 2001.

> This Caldecott Award winner shows what happened after the wolf blew the first pig right out of the story.

## THE TORTOISE AND THE HARE

Lowell, Susan. *The Tortoise and the Jackrabbit.* Illustrated by Jim Harris. Northland, 1994.

> Jackrabbit snoozes under a mesquite tree, which allows the tortoise to win.

Sykes, Julie. *That's Not Fair, Hare!* Illustrated by Tim Warnes. Barron's Educational Series, 2001.

> Rabbit wins the first race but loses the rematch to race home (turtle wins by pulling his head in his shell).

Vozar, David. *M. C. Turtle and the Hip Hop Hare: A Happenin' Rap.* Illustrated by Betsy Lewin. Doubleday, 1995.

> M. C. stands for "mostly crawling." Hare loses the race because he dances when he should have run.

## THE TWELVE PRINCESSES

Pancheri, Jan. *The Twelve Poodle Princesses.* Hutchinson, 1996.

> This version features an all-dog cast.

## SEVERAL FOLKLORE CHARACTERS IN ONE STORY

Ada, Alma Flor. *Dear Peter Rabbit.* Illustrated by Leslie Tryon. Atheneum, 1994.

> Peter Rabbit, Goldilocks, and others correspond.

Ada, Alma Flor. *With Love, Little Red Hen.* Illustrated by Leslie Tryon. Atheneum, 2001.

> The folkore characters try to help Ms. Hen while two wolves plot to eat her.

Ada, Alma Flor. *Yours Truly, Goldilocks.* Illustrated by Leslie Tryon. Atheneum. 1998.

The three little pigs invite Baby Bear, Goldilocks, and others to their housewarming party.

Ahlberg, Janet, and Allan Ahlberg. *Each Peach Pear Plum.* Viking, 1978.

I spy with my little eye several folklore characters.

Ahlberg, Janet, and Allan Ahlberg. *The Jolly Christmas Postman.* Little, Brown, 1991.

The postman delivers holiday cards and gifts to Mr. H. Dumpty, R. Hood, and others.

Ahlberg, Janet, and Allan Ahlberg. *The Jolly Postman.* Little, Brown, 1986.

The postman delivers letters to several familiar storybook characters.

Child, Lauren. *Beware of the Storybook Wolves.* Scholastic, 2001.

A couple of wolves, a witch, and a fairy godmother leave their stories to visit (and menace) a little boy.

Dealey, Erin. *Goldie Locks Has Chicken Pox.* Illustrated by Hanako Wakiyama. Atheneum, 2002.

Several folklore characters visit poor Goldie, who, on top of chicken pox, suffers from a bratty brother.

Grindley, Sally. *Who Is It?* Illustrated by Rosalind Beardshaw. Peachtree, 2000.

Someone's eating the porridge. Who is it? Kids answer clues about several folklore characters.

Little, Jean, and Maggie de Vries. *Once Upon a Golden Apple.* Illustrated by Phoebe Gilman. Viking, 1991.

Kids get upset when Dad mixes up his fairy tales.

McNaughton, Colin. *Oops!* Harcourt, 1997.

A wolf is involved in a combination of Little Red Riding Hood and the Three Little Pigs.

Prater, John, and Vivian French. *Once Upon a Time.* Candlewick, 1993.

A boy's world is populated by several folktale characters.

Rae, Jennifer. *Dog Tales*. Illustrated by Rose Cowles. Scholastic, 1999.

A dog retells several stories, such as Jack Russell and the Beanstalk.

Scieszka, Jon. *The Stinky Cheese Man and Other Fairly Stupid Tales*. Illustrated by Lane Smith. Viking, 1992.

Everything we ever knew about traditional literature is turned upside down.

Vozar, David. *Yo, Hungry Wolf!: A Nursery Rap*. Illustrated by Betsy Lewin. Doubleday, 1993.

A wolf finds himself rapping through The Three Little Pigs, Little Red Riding Hood, and The Boy Who Cried Wolf.

## Story Collections

Ahlberg, Allan. *Ten in a Bed*. Kestrel, 1989.

Several folklore characters demand bedtime stories.

Brooke, William J. *Teller of Tales*. HarperCollins, 1994.

Stories include "Gold in Locks" and "Little Well-Read Riding Hood."

Brooke, William J. *A Telling of the Tales*. HarperCollins, 1990.

Retellings include a Sleeping Beauty who demands identification from the prince who allegedly woke her with a kiss.

Brooke, William J. *Untold Tales*. HarperCollins, 1992.

Contains retellings of The Frog Prince, Snow White, Beauty and the Beast, and Sleeping Beauty.

King-Smith, Dick. *Hogsel and Gruntel: And Other Animal Stories*. Illustrated by Michael Terry. Orchard, 1999.

Stories include "Little Red Riding Pig" and "Goldipig and the Three Bears."

Lansky, Bruce. *Newfangled Fairy Tales: Classic Stories with a Funny Twist: Book #1*. Meadowbrook, 1997.

Stories include "Little Bad Wolf and Red Riding Hood," "Jill and the Beanstalk," and "The Prince and the Pea."

## Songs

**HUSH LITTLE BABY**

Kirk, Daniel. *Hush Little Alien*. Hyperion, 1999.

"If that shooting star's too hot, Papa's going to find you an astronaut."

**OLD MACDONALD HAD A FARM**

Barrett, Judi. *Old MacDonald Had an Apartment House*. Illustrated by Ron Barrett. Atheneum, 1969.

An apartment house gets turned into a farm.

Palatini, Maggie. *Piggie Pie*. Illustrated by Howard Fine. Clarion, 1995.

Gritch the Witch heads over the river and through the woods to Old MacDonald's farm to grab eight plump pigs for her piggie pie.

**THERE WAS AN OLD LADY WHO SWALLOWED A FLY**

Jackson, Alison. *I Know an Old Lady Who Swallowed a Pie*. Illustrated by Judith Byron Schachner. Dutton, 1997.

An old lady comes over for a Thanksgiving dinner, eats the entire meal, and winds up as a holiday parade float.

Sloat, Teri. *There Was an Old Lady Who Swallowed a Trout*. Illustrated by Reynolds Ruffins. Holt, 1998.

This version, set in the Pacific Northwest, finds the old lady swallowing all kinds of marine life before gulping down the ocean.

**'TWAS THE NIGHT BEFORE CHRISTMAS**

Pilkey, Dav. *'Twas the Night Before Thanksgiving*. Orchard, 1990.

"He whistled and shouted / And called them by name: / 'Now Ollie, now Stanley, now Larry and Moe, / On Wally, on Beaver, on Shemp and Groucho!'"

**THE WHEELS ON THE BUS**

Hort, Lenny. *The Seals on the Bus*. Illustrated by G. Brian Karas. Holt, 2000.

The seals go "erp, erp, erp," the tigers go "roar, roar, roar," and the humans go "help, help, help!"

## Reader's Theater and Drama Scripts

Fredericks, Anthony D. *Frantic Frogs and Other Frankly Fractured Folktales for Reader's Theater.* Teacher Ideas Press, 1993.

Fredericks, Anthony D. *Silly Salamanders and Other Slightly Stupid Stuff for Reader's Theater.* Teacher Ideas Press, 2000.

Fredericks, Anthony D. *Tadpole Tales and Other Totally Terrific Treats for Reader's Theater.* Teacher Ideas Press, 1997.

# EASY READERS

Bonsall, Crosby. *And I Mean It Stanley.* HarperCollins, 1974.

A little kid spends the entire book yelling and taunting the unseen Stanley. This spare, realistic monologue hits the nail on the head and always makes me laugh.

Bonsall, Crosby. *The Day I Had to Play with My Sister.* HarperCollins, 1972.

This is a quietly amusing story about a boy trying his hardest to teach his younger sister how to play hide-and-seek. The illustrations of the frustrated boy and his sister's innocence bring out the humor.

Cazet, Denys. *Minnie and Moo Go to the Moon.* Dorling Kindersley, 1998.

Two cows try to drive the farmer's tractor. They believe the secret to driving lies in wearing the farmer's hat and repeating the magic words, "You cheesy piece of junk! You broken-down, no-good, rusty bucket of bolts!" The illustration that made me laugh hardest was one of the cows performing a side-vault over a fence to elude the farmer. Sequels: *Minnie and Moo Go Dancing* (Dorling Kindersley, 1998); *Minnie and Moo and the Thanksgiving Tree* (Dorling Kindersley, 1998); *Minnie and Moo Go to Paris* (Dorling Kindersley, 1999); *Minnie and Moo Save the Earth* (Dorling Kindersley, 1999); *Minnie and Moo and the Musk of Zorro* (Dorling Kindersley, 2000); *Minnie and Moo Meet Frankenswine* (HarperCollins, 2001); *Minnie and Moo and the Potato from Planet X* (HarperCollins, 2002).

Eastman, P. D. *Flap Your Wings.* Random, 1969.

Mr. and Mrs. Bird unwittingly hatch an alligator egg. They try to keep up with the youngster's hunger by bringing it fruit, bugs, and worms, but

"Junior never stopped eating." The alligator soon becomes too big for the nest and the Birds encourage it to fly away.

Karlin, Nurit. *The Fat Cat Sat on the Mat.* HarperCollins, 1996.

Lots of fun assonance as a rat, bat, and hat try to get the fat cat off the mat. When they all leave, the mat says, "Thank goodness."

Kessler, Leonard. *Old Turtle's Baseball Stories.* Greenwillow, 1982.

Turtle tells stories about former baseball greats such as Cleo Octopus, who threw a "fast ball, slow ball, curve ball, and knuckle ball" all at the same time. Sequel: *Old Turtle's Winter Games* (Greenwillow, 1983).

LeSieg, Theo. *I Wish That I Had Duck Feet.* Random, 1965.

A boy uses his imagination to think of the benefits and disadvantages of having duck feet, two deer horns, a whale spout, a long tail, and an elephant nose. LeSieg is Geisel spelled backward. Geisel is Dr. Seuss's real name. Share this trivia tidbit with your audience.

Lobel, Arnold. *Frog and Toad Are Friends.* HarperCollins, 1970.

This volume contains five classic short, short stories featuring the two friends. "The Story" shows Toad thinking of a story to tell to Frog. However, he has trouble creating one. He paces, stands on his head, and dumps a glass of water in hopes that these actions will help him think of a story. Instead, his crazy efforts become the story. Sequels: *Frog and Toad Together* (HarperCollins, 1972); *Frog and Toad All Year* (HarperCollins, 1976); *Days with Frog and Toad* (HarperCollins, 1979).

Lobel, Arnold. *Grasshopper on the Road.* HarperCollins, 1978.

Grasshopper has many encounters with insects and worms. The funniest occurs when he meets the "We Love Morning Club." He gets kicked out when he admits, "I love afternoon, too."

Marshall, Edward. *Fox on Wheels.* Illustrated by James Marshall. Dial, 1983.

There are several short books featuring Fox. This one in particular contains great dialogue. String several of the Fox stories together for a reader's theater presentation. The story "Fox and the Grapes" contains one of the funniest lines. Fox is taunted to join Millie high up in a tree. When he finally gets up, she tells him that she doesn't know how to get down. Fox replies, "Well, that's just dandy!" Companion books: *Fox and His Friends* (Dial, 1982); *Fox at School* (Dial, 1983); *Fox All Week* (Dial,

1984); *Fox on the Job* (Dial, 1988); *Fox Be Nimble* (Dial, 1990); *Fox Outfoxed* (Dial, 1992); *Fox on Stage* (Dial, 1993).

Marshall, Edward. *Three by the Sea.* Illustrated by James Marshall. Dial, 1981.

Three friends tell each other stories. They think each other's stories are dumb. They are, but they're funny, too. The best one is about a rat who buys a cat from a pet store. The cat starts feeling hungry. Hmmm, what do cats like to eat? Another piece of trivia you can pass onto your audience is that Edward Marshall is really James Marshall. Sequel: *Four on the Shore* (Dial, 1985).

Palmer, Helen. *A Fish Out of Water.* Illustrated by P. D. Eastman. Random, 1961.

A boy feeds his new pet goldfish the whole box of fish food despite the pet store owner's warnings. The fish immediately outgrows the goldfish bowl, then the vase, various pots, the bathtub, the flooded cellar, and the city swimming pool. Helen Palmer was Dr. Seuss's first wife. More Dr. Seuss trivia to share with your audience.

Parish, Peggy. *Amelia Bedelia.* HarperCollins, 1963.

Amelia Bedelia's first day on the job has her dusting the furniture (by putting dust all over the furniture), putting out the lights (which she accomplishes by gathering all of the lightbulbs in the house and hanging them on the clothesline), and dressing the chicken (she makes an outfit for the evening's main entrée.) Luckily for her, she makes a mean lemon meringue pie. Amelia Bedelia appears in over a dozen sequels, some written by Peggy Parish's nephew, Herman Parish.

Quackenbush, Robert. *Henry's Awful Mistake.* Parent's Magazine, 1980.

Henry the Duck sees an ant in his kitchen. Not wanting his aunt to think that his house isn't clean, he chases the ant. In the process, he moves the stove, smashes a hole in the wall, breaks a water pipe, and floods his house, which washes away. Settled in his new house, he sees an ant. . . .

Rylant, Cynthia. *Mr. Putter and Tabby Pick the Pears.* Illustrated by Arthur Howard. Harcourt, 1995.

Mr. Putter's cranky legs, cranky knees, and cranky feet lead him to make a slingshot out of his poodle underwear. He uses it to shoot the apples that have already fallen on the ground at the pears in the pear tree.

Companion books: *Mr. Putter and Tabby Walk the Dog* (Harcourt, 1994); *Mr. Putter and Tabby Bake the Cake* (Harcourt, 1994); *Mr. Putter and Tabby Pour the Tea* (Harcourt, 1994).

Seuss, Dr. *The Cat in the Hat.* Random, 1957.

The book that revolutionized the genre of easy readers is still funny to today's young generation. The world-famous cat (who wears the world's most recognizable hat) brings Thing One and Thing Two over to the house one boring, rainy day while Mother was away. Sequel: *The Cat in the Hat Comes Back* (Random, 1957).

Seuss, Dr. *Green Eggs and Ham.* Random, 1960.

Sam offers green eggs and ham in a variety of ways to the narrator in this classic easy reader. Only one word in the text has more than one syllable. Many librarians have served green food with this book over the years.

Seuss, Dr. *One Fish Two Fish Red Fish Blue Fish.* Random, 1960.

Several short hilarious episodes introduce the reader to the Zans (they're good for opening cans), the seven hump Wump, sheep walking in their sleep, a boxing Gox, and a singing Ying (among other things). Why is this book so funny? "I don't know. Go ask your Pop."

Smith, Lane. *The Happy Hocky Family.* Viking, 1993.

This parody of early easy reader primers will appeal to older kids and adults more than the easy reading crowd, despite the childlike illustrations. Use it as a writing exercise. The funniest bits involve the baby with the red balloon, which turns into the baby with the string, and the child with the ant farm talking about "responsibility." The ants are seen loose all over the next story.

Thomas, Shelley Moore. *Good Night, Good Knight.* Illustrated by Jennifer Plecas. Dutton, 2000.

Three little dragons keep a brave knight busy as he unwittingly answers their calls for tuck-ins, drinks of water, reading, singing, and good-night kisses.

Wiseman, Bernard. *Morris and Boris.* Dodd, 1974.

A moose and a bear have three series of hilarious and exasperating dialogues. "The Riddles," "The Tongue-Twisters," and "The Game" are perfect stories for reader's theater. Morris appears by himself and at times with Boris in nearly a dozen companion books.

## JUVENILE FICTION CHAPTER BOOKS

Avi. *Romeo and Juliet Together (and Alive!) at Last.* Orchard, 1987.

Pete Saltz has a crush on Anabell Stackpoole. Pete's friends consort to have the two play Romeo and Juliet in a school drama club's production. Read aloud chapter 18, where "Romeo" asks his friend's advice on the kissing scene. He's concerned that "Juliet" may spit or burp during the kiss. Also fun to read aloud is the scene in chapter 31, where "Juliet" struggles onstage to uncork her "vial of poison."

Blume, Judy. *Superfudge.* Dutton, 1980.

Every page of this book contains hilarious accounts of Peter; his brother, Fudge; their new sister, Tootsie; their friends; and their parents. There are many scenes you could read to book-talk this book. I'm partial to the second half of chapter 6, titled "Farley Drexel Meets Rat Face." Fudge has a confrontation with his new kindergarten teacher because she won't call him Fudge. Companion books: *Tales of a Fourth Grade Nothing* (Dutton, 1972); *Fudge-a-Mania* (Dutton, 1990).

Cleary, Beverly. *Ramona the Pest.* Morrow, 1968.

Ramona Quimby shines in the spotlight in her first solo book after appearing in the Henry Huggins series and with her sister in *Beezus and Ramona.* The first chapter, "Ramona's Great Day," is a classic. She anxiously expects a present after her teacher instructs her to "sit here for the present." She also learns a new song about "the dawnzer lee light," wonders aloud how Mike Mulligan goes to the bathroom while digging a hole in *Mike Mulligan and His Steam Shovel,* gets into trouble by grabbing Susan's hair with the "boing-boing curls," and makes the other kids giggle with her snoring noises during rest time. Sequels: *Ramona the Brave* (Morrow, 1975); *Ramona and Her Father* (Morrow, 1977); *Ramona and Her Mother* (Morrow, 1979); *Ramona Quimby, Age 8* (Morrow, 1981); *Ramona, Forever* (Morrow, 1984).

Clements, Andrew. *Frindle.* Simon & Schuster, 1996.

Even though this book is a sensitive and touching tribute to teachers everywhere, it has its humorous moments. Nick butts heads with his fifth-grade teacher, Mrs. Granger, a no-nonsense instructor everyone is sure has X-ray vision. Read chapter 3, when Mrs. Granger turns one of Nick's favorite tricks back on him. "Frindle" is a term Nick coins for "pen," much to the teacher's annoyance.

Coville, Bruce. *Aliens Ate My Homework*. Minstrel, 1993.

Rod finds himself helping miniature aliens apprehend an interstellar criminal—the father of a classmate. The aliens call Rod's little siblings "larvae." They land their spacecraft in Rod's papier-mâché mixture and eat his volcano science project, leaving him to plead to his teacher that "aliens ate my homework."

Cutler, Jane. *No Dogs Allowed*. Farrar, 1992.

Five-year-old Edward got so involved in pretending he was a dog that eventually he "was Edward about half of the time, and the other half, he was Truffles." Read aloud this title chapter, the chapter in which Edward and his brother get glasses for the first time, or "Killer Kelly," in which Edward befriends a supposed bully.

Dahl, Roald. *The BFG*. Farrar, 1982.

Any book in which the reader can say words like "snozzcumber," "frobscottle," "fleshlumpeater," and "whizzpopper" has to be funny. The Big Friendly Giant's entire dialogue is a hoot to read aloud. The chapter titled "Frobscottle and Whizzpoppers" is delightfully naughty to share.

Dahl, Roald. *Matilda*. Viking, 1988.

Matilda must face the mean Miss Trunchbull and her idiotic parents who think reading is a waste of time. Matilda's father is a used-car salesman who brags to the family how well he cheats his customers. After he insults Matilda one too many times, she gets her revenge by putting glue in his hat. Read this hilarious chapter, titled "The Hat and the Superglue."

Dahl, Roald. *The Twits*. Illustrated by Quentin Blake. Knopf, 1981.

Mr. Twit is a mean, hairy-faced man who hasn't washed his bristly nailbrushy face for years. Mrs. Twit is just as horrid. They play nasty tricks on each other, catch birds with sticky glue and bake them in bird pies, and mistreat a family of monkeys. Create reader's theater scripts out of the mean trick chapters, such as "The Glass Eye," "The Frog," "The Wormy Spaghetti," and "Mrs. Twit Has the Shrinks."

Erickson, John D. *Hank the Cowdog*. Maverick, 1983.

Hank is the head of ranch security. He's hilarious as he brags about the goings-on at his ranch and his importance in the scheme of things—from barking back at the coyotes, causing his human to fire a gun in his direction, to going to town and insulting the dog in the next pickup truck. More than thirty Hank the Cowdog books have been published to date.

Fitzgerald, John D. *The Great Brain*. Dial, 1967.

Set in 1896 Utah, the book will grab the attention of every young reader when the first indoor toilet arrives at the home of Tom, the Great Brain. Tom charges admission for kids to watch grumpy Mr. Harvey dig up their backyard for the cesspool. Then Tom's father gets very angry when everyone in town shows up to watch them uncrate the toilet in the middle of Main Street. "This is the thing-a-mah-bob you sit on!" Sequels: *More Adventures of the Great Brain* (Dial, 1969); *Me and My Little Brain* (Dial, 1971); *The Great Brain at the Academy* (Dial, 1972); *The Great Brain Reforms* (Dial, 1973); *The Return of the Great Brain* (Dial, 1974); *The Great Brain Does It Again* (Dial, 1975); *The Great Brain Is Back* (Dial, 1995).

Fleischman, Sid. *McBroom's Almanac*. Little, Brown, 1984.

All of Fleischman's tall-tale McBroom books are hilarious. McBroom is a farmer who owns a one-acre farm that contains the richest soil around. His almanac contains all types of wisdom such as "How to Keep Warm All Winter with One Stick of Wood" and whoppers about the size of mosquitoes. Share bits and pieces of the almanac throughout the year in programs, on bulletin boards, and in library fliers. Example: "January is a bad month to paint your barn." This is also a good source if you host a Liars' Club. The McBroom books have been recently repackaged and released as the following: *McBroom's Wonderful One-Acre Farm: Three Tales* (Greenwillow, 1997); *Here Comes McBroom: Three More Tall Tales* (Greenwillow, 1998); *McBroom's Ghost* (Little, Brown, 1998); *McBroom Tells the Truth* (Price Stern, 1998); *McBroom Tells a Lie* (Price Stern, 1999); *McBroom the Rainmaker* (Little, Brown, 1999).

Hale, Bruce. *The Chameleon Wore Chartreuse: From the Casebook of Chet Gecko, Private Eye*. Harcourt, 2000.

These reptilian narratives read like classic detective novels. Chet, a student and amateur detective, eats peanut-butter-and-ladybug sandwiches and solves crimes. The stories are filled with puns. "Shirley coughed, 'I can afford fifty cents a day.' 'Shirley, you jest,' I replied." Sequels: *The Mystery of Mr. Nice* (Harcourt, 2000); *The Big Nap* (Harcourt, 2001); *Farewell, My Lunch Bag* (Harcourt, 2001); *The Hamster of the Baskervilles* (Harcourt, 2002).

Horvath, Polly. *The Trolls.* Farrar, 1999.

Mr. and Mrs. Anderson are forced to ask eccentric Aunt Polly to watch Melissa, Amanda, and Peter after the children's regular sitter comes down with the bubonic plague. Read the chapter titled "Greens" aloud. It is one of the funniest selections in children's literature. Aunt Polly plays with her green beans while spinning a story about Uncle Edward and great-uncle Louis "who came for two weeks and stayed for six years." The children, who detest beans, find themselves craving the vegetables after seeing Aunt Polly knitting with them, making walrus tusks, and dropping them in her mouth like a clothespin-in-a-bottle game.

Howe, Deborah, and James Howe. *Bunnicula: A Rabbit-Tale of Mystery.* Atheneum, 1979.

Harold, the family dog, narrates the story of Chester the cat and a new-comer to the family, a bunny named Bunnicula. When white vegetables, drained of their juice, appear in the house, Chester is convinced that Bunnicula is a vampire rabbit. The climax comes when Chester, who can read, substitutes a piece of steak to drive through the bunny, instead of a wooden stake. Sequels: *Howliday Inn* (Atheneum, 1982); *The Celery Stalks at Midnight* (Atheneum, 1983); *Nighty-Nightmare* (Atheneum, 1987); *Return to Howliday Inn* (Atheneum, 1992).

Hurwitz, Johanna. *The Adventures of Ali Baba Bernstein.* Morrow, 1985.

David Bernstein keeps track of his age by year, month, and day. He also renames himself after learning there are four Davids in his classroom and seventeen David Bernsteins in the phone book. He eventually invites them over to an all–David Bernstein party. Sequels: *Hurray for Ali Baba Bernstein* (Morrow, 1989); *Ali Baba Bernstein, Lost and Found* (Morrow, 1992).

Juster, Norton. *The Phantom Tollbooth.* Random, 1961.

The opening chapter is a great hook to introduce kids to one of the word-play classics. Milo is unhappy and bored with life until he sees the tollbooth for the first time and goes on the ride of his life. "Results are not guaranteed, but if not perfectly satisfied, your wasted time will be refunded."

King-Smith, Dick. *Ace, the Very Important Pig.* Crown, 1990.

A young pig is saved from going to the market by his ability to understand every word Farmer Tubbs says. Read the chapter "A Pig and a Cat," in which Ace learns the term "housebroken" as well as the names of the cows and sheep (the sheep are all named Barbara or "Baaaabaara").

Lowry, Lois. *All About Sam.* Houghton Mifflin, 1988.

The first in the series about Anastasia Krupnik's younger brother begins with newborn Sam. Read the part of the first chapter that describes how Sam hates his hat: "I hate this hat," he would yell, but his family only heard "Waaahhhh." Follow up by reading the first half of the second chapter, which describes how Sam tries to get his family to "do the blurble blurble thing." Sequels: *Attaboy, Sam!* (Houghton Mifflin, 1992); *See You Around, Sam!* (Houghton Mifflin, 1996); *Zooman Sam* (Houghton Mifflin, 1999).

Lowry, Lois. *Anastasia Krupnik.* Houghton Mifflin, 1979.

Anastasia has a list of things she loves ("my wart," "my name," "making lists") and things she hates ("boys," "liver"). Read chapter 5, in which Anastasia asks her parents why they gave her that name. Sequels: *Anastasia Again* (Houghton Mifflin, 1981); *Anastasia at Your Service* (Houghton Mifflin, 1982); *Anastasia, Ask Your Analyst* (Houghton Mifflin, 1984); *Anastasia on Her Own* (Houghton Mifflin, 1985); *Anastasia Has the Answers* (Houghton Mifflin, 1986); *Anastasia's Chosen Career* (Houghton Mifflin, 1987); *Anastasia at This Address* (Houghton Mifflin, 1991); *Anastasia, Absolutely* (Houghton Mifflin, 1995).

MacDonald, Betty. *Mrs. Piggle-Wiggle.* Lippincott, 1947.

Mrs. Piggle-Wiggle lives in an upside-down house and knows a lot about children. She helps parents around town with various cures to typical child problems, such as the "Won't-Pick-Up-Toys Cure," the "Never-Want-to-Go-to-Bedders-Cure," and the "Slow-Eater-Tiny-Bite-Taker-Cure." Read aloud "The Radish Cure" in which Patsy refuses to take a bath. "I haaaaaaaaaaaate baaaaaaaaths!" Sequels: *Mrs. Piggle-Wiggle's*

*Magic* (Lippincott, 1949); *Mrs. Piggle-Wiggle's Farm* (Lippincott, 1954); and *Hello, Mrs. Piggle-Wiggle* (Lippincott, 1957).

Manes, Stephen. *Be a Perfect Person in Just Three Days.* Clarion, 1982.

You must wear a stalk of broccoli around your neck, fast for a day, and do absolutely nothing for another twenty-four hours in order to become a perfect person, according to the instructions of Dr. Silverfish. Read the opening chapter, which contains a lot of interaction between the author and Milo, the young protagonist.

McKay, Hilary. *Dog Friday.* Margaret K. McElderry, 1994.

Robin has a fear of dogs that is cured partially by the new, wild family next door. Robin's mother runs a dilapidated bed-and-breakfast and has a love-hate relationship with her boarders. "If I ever start behaving like a bed and breakfaster . . . break it to me gently, Robin, and I will do the decent thing and fling myself off the cliffs." Read aloud sections of chapter 5, where Robin's mother is out and two new guests are served by the neighbor kids.

Milne, A. A. *Winnie-the-Pooh.* Dutton, 1926.

Pooh getting stuck in the hole while Rabbit hangs his wash on Pooh's "south end," hunting for woozles, meeting the heffelump—these memorable scenes secure Pooh's place as one of the most enduring children's books for all ages. Companion book: *The House at Pooh Corner* (Dutton, 1928).

Park, Barbara. *Junie B. Jones and the Stupid Smelly Bus.* Random, 1992.

This is the first in a series of books about the funniest kindergartner since Ramona Quimby. There are over a dozen books in the series. Pick any chapter from any book and you'll get laughs.

Park, Barbara. *Skinnybones.* Random, 1982.

Barbara Park is one of our funniest children's writers, and *Skinnybones* is one of her funniest. Alex has a very big mouth, which lands him in all kinds of trouble. In the first chapter, his mother catches him in a lie. ("If you were Pinocchio . . . we could saw off your nose and have enough firewood to last the winter.") During a baseball game near the end of the book, Alex reaches first base only because he shouts "Booga Booga" at the first baseman. Sequel: *Almost Starring Skinnybones* (Random, 1988).

Peck, Richard. *A Long Way from Chicago.* Dial, 1998.

Meet Grandma Dowdel, one of the most outrageous senior citizens in children's literature. She constantly fights for the underdog by facing up to a gang of bullies and besting a crooked sheriff. Her grandchildren spend summers with her in this series of short stories set in rural Depression-era Illinois. Read aloud the chapter titled "Shotgun Cheatham's Last Night Above Ground," in which Grandma Dowdel succeeds in scaring a city newspaper reporter and brings honor to one of the locals. This funny short story can be found in Harry Mazer's collection *Twelve Shots: Stories About Guns* (Delacorte, 1997). Sequel: *A Year Down Yonder* (Dial, 2000).

Peck, Robert Newton. *Soup.* Knopf, 1974.

Soup and Rob manage to make a lot of mischief in 1920s rural Vermont. Read the chapter titled "Apples and Mrs. Stetson," in which the boys break a stained glass window of a church and old Mrs. Stetson chugs up the hill after them. Soup and Rob appear in over a dozen sequels plus the spin-off series Little Soup.

Pinkwater, Daniel Manus. *Blue Moose.* Dodd, 1975.

Mr. Breton is pleased when a blue moose shows up at his restaurant and compliments his oyster stew. The moose immediately becomes the head waiter and encourages the restaurant customers to compliment the chef. Then the game warden shows up. This absurd tale is short enough to read in one sitting. Sequels: *Return of the Moose* (Dodd, 1979); *The Moospire* (Dodd, 1986).

Pullman, Philip. *I Was a Rat!* Knopf, 2000.

One of Cinderella's rats is transformed into a boy and stays that way. We meet him as he meets an old couple and constantly repeats, "I was a rat." The laughs come when he lapses into his old rat habits, such as chewing on a pencil or a not-so-nice lady's hand. Copies of the local newspaper, *The Daily Scourge,* are scattered throughout the story, adding to the humor.

Robinson, Barbara. *The Best Christmas Pageant Ever.* HarperCollins, 1972.

The opening line will hook the kids and not let them go: "The Herdmans were absolutely the worst kids in the history of the world." This tough bunch decide to take part in the church's annual Christmas pageant, which will be directed by the narrator's mother. Caution: If you read the first chapter to a group of kids, they will not allow you to stop. Sequel: *The Best School Year Ever* (HarperCollins, 1994).

Rockwell, Thomas. *How to Eat Fried Worms.* Watts, 1973.

A group of boys bet Billy that he can't eat fifteen worms for $50. This story is deliciously gross. Read the chapter titled "The Ninth Worm," where Billy is served a suspiciously long worm (his rivals glued two worms together). Remember to serve those gummy worms afterward.

Sachar, Louis. *Dogs Don't Tell Jokes.* Knopf, 1991.

Smart-alecky Gary "Goon" Boone works very hard to be funny. Read chapter 5, which shows Goon hard at work developing a stand-up comedy routine. Sachar throws in an inside joke with a reference to Goon having a copy of Sachar's *Sideways Arithmetic from Wayside School,* "which he didn't understand."

Seidler, Tor. *Mean Margaret.* HarperCollins, 1997.

The mean ninth child in the family is dumped in the woods by her older siblings. A pair of woodchucks take her in. Read the chapter titled "A Direct Hit," in which a skunk sprays Margaret after she stomps on his tail.

Smith, Janice Lee. *The Monster in the Third Drawer and Other Stories About Adam Joshua.* HarperCollins, 1981.

Adam Joshua grumpily handles the changes in his life (moving and a new baby sister) in touching, yet humorous ways. Share the second half of the chapter titled "Amanda Jane Moves In," where Adam Joshua writes "will be leaving soon" on his sister's diaper bottom. Adam Joshua appears in several sequels.

Spinelli, Jerry. *Who Put That Hair in My Toothbrush?* Little, Brown, 1984.

Two siblings—Megamouth Megin and Grosso Greg—constantly argue. They give their sides of the story by narrating alternating chapters. Pick any of their many confrontations to read aloud. Start with the opening chapter, where Greg pays their younger brother to flush the toilet while Megin is in the shower.

Whybrow, Ian. *Little Wolf's Book of Badness.* Carolrhoda, 1999.

Little Wolf is sent to Uncle Bigbad's Cunning College, set in the deep woods of Frettnin Forest, to learn the rules of badness. These rules include "huff and puff a lot," "say lots of rude words," "fib your head off," and "if it squeaks, eat it." Little Wolf's funny observations are delivered in the form of letters back to his mom and dad. Sequels: *Little Wolf's Diary of Daring Deeds* (Carolrhoda, 2000); *Little Wolf's Haunted Hall for Small Horrors* (Carolrhoda, 2000); *Little Wolf, Forest Detective* (Carolrhoda, 2001).

## POETRY COLLECTIONS

Booth, David. *Doctor Knickerbocker and Other Rhymes.* Illustrated by Maryann Kovalski. Ticknor & Fields, 1993.

This collection of traditional schoolyard chants ranges from "Jingle bells / Batman smells / Robin laid an egg" to "Mary had a little lamb. / Her father shot it dead. / And now it goes to school with her / Between two chunks of bread."

Brown, Calef. *Polka-Bats and Octopus Slacks: 14 Stories.* Houghton Mifflin, 1998.

These absurd, sometimes macabre, short-short stories are told in verse. "Ed" has cherries on his head and eventually attracts flies, "The Lonely Surfer" is lonely because he surfs in the desert, and "Polka-bats" do gross things on people's heads. The poem "Funky Snowman" knocked a classroom full of adults to the floor with laughter when one local teacher punctuated the line, "Kick it, Funky Snowman!!"

Ciardi, John. *The Hopeful Trout and Other Limericks.* Illustrated by Susan Meddaugh. Houghton Mifflin, 1989.

Ciardi, a master of limericks, includes verses about a nervous worm that ties itself in knots and two old geezers who are forced to pull porcupine quills out of their sneezers with tweezers.

Cole, William. *Oh, How Silly!* Viking, 1970.

This volume contains the hilarious poem "Two Witches," in which one witch has an itch and the other a twitch. Companion books: *Oh, What Nonsense!* (Viking, 1966); *Oh, Such Foolishness!* (Viking, 1978).

Cole, Willam. *Poem Stew.* Illustrated by Karen Ann Weinhaus. Lippincott, 1981.

Cole collected several funny food poems, including "Rhinoceros Stew"—

one needs to "chew it and chew it and chew it"; "Speak Clearly," in which a father admonishes his child not to talk with a mouthful of food; and the classic anonymous chant: "Get up, get up, you lazy-head, / Get up you lazy sinner, / We need those sheets for tablecloths, / It's nearly time for dinner!"

Cole, William. *A Zooful of Animals*. Illustrated by Lynn Munsinger. Houghton Mifflin, 1992.

This collection of poems covers both common and unusual animals such as hyenas, the platypus, llamas, skunks, and pygmy elephants. The funniest illustration is a double-page spread showing what happens when you try to gift-wrap an elephant.

Dakos, Kalli. *If You're Not Here, Please Raise Your Hand: Poems About School*. Illustrated by G. Brian Karas. Simon & Schuster, 1990.

Dakos hit the market with several collections of school humor poetry. Companion books: *Don't Read This Book, Whatever You Do: More Poems About School* (Simon & Schuster, 1993); *Mrs. Cole on an Onion Roll* (Simon & Schuster, 1995); *The Goof Who Invented Homework* (Dial, 1996); *The Bug in Teacher's Coffee* (HarperCollins, 1999).

Florian, Douglas. *Beast Feast*. Harcourt, 1994.

Florian's very short animal poems are funny and right on target, as they are in the companion volumes: *On the Wing* (Harcourt, 1996); *Insectlopedia* (Harcourt, 1997); *In the Swim* (Harcourt, 1997); *Mammalabilia* (Harcourt, 2000); *Lizards, Frogs, and Polliwogs* (Harcourt, 2001).

Florian, Douglas. *Laugh-eteria*. Penguin, 1999.

This collection starts with a test poem before the title page and ends with an alien lullaby in which an alien is encouraged to lay down its many heads. In between are poems about a unicorn with its horn on its behind, an aunteater that eats aunts instead of ants, and a hot dog with the works (truly everything on it).

Grossman, Bill. *Timothy Tunny Swallowed a Bunny*. Illustrated by Kevin Hawkes. HarperCollins, 2000.

This collection of weird characters, such as Old Ned, who walks with a horse on his head, and Kevin T. Moses, who has seventeen noses, is highlighted by the poem "The Barber," in which a customer's ears are lopped off and he looks up at the barber's shriek and says, "What?"

Heide, Florence Parry. *Grim and Ghastly Goings-On*. Illustrated by Victoria Chess. Lothrop, 1992.

This collection features monsters that are more silly than scary. The classic poem "What You Don't Know About Food" gives us food origins (jelly is from jellyfish and it's true that spaghetti is made from worms).

Hoberman, Mary Ann. *Yellow Butter Purple Jelly Red Jam Black Bread*. Illustrated by Chaya Bernstein. Viking, 1981.

The title poem always gets a laugh when I read it aloud, especially the lines read as if your mouth is full. Other highlights of this, one of my favorite poetry collections, include "Waiters" and "Brother."

Katz, Alan. *Take Me Out of the Bathtub and Other Silly Dilly Songs*. Illustrated by David Catrow. Margaret K. McElderry, 2001.

Fourteen sets of irreverent lyrics are set to the melodies of popular songs. "I've Been Cleaning Up My Bedroom" is set to the tune of "I've Been Working on the Railroad," "Stinky, Stinky Diaper Change" is set to "Twinkle, Twinkle, Little Star," and "Give Me a Break," set to "Home on the Range," is a complaint about having an overdue library book.

Lansky, Bruce. *Kids Pick the Funniest Poems*. Meadowbrook, 1991.

Lansky has compiled some of the funniest and most popular poetry collections of the 1990s. Companion books: *A Bad Case of the Giggles: Kids Pick the Funniest Poems, Book #2* (Meadowbrook, 1994); *Poetry Party* (Meadowbrook, 1996); *No More Homework! No More Tests: Kids' Favorite Funny School Poems* (Meadowbrook, 1997); *Happy Birthday to Me: Kids Pick the Funniest Birthday Poems* (Meadowbrook, 1998); *Miles of Smiles: Kids Pick the Funniest Poems, Book #3* (Meadowbrook, 1998); *If Pigs Could Fly and Other Deep Thoughts* (Meadowbrook, 2000).

Lee, Dennis. *Alligator Pie*. Illustrated by Frank Newfeld. Macmillan, 1974.

This landmark collection of original poems contains "Willoughby Wallaby Woo" and the poem I call the world's toughest tongue twister, "The Sitter and the Butter and the Better Batter Fritter." Encourage kids to make new verses to the title poem, such as "Alligator Spaghetti / Alligator Spaghetti / If I don't get some, I think I'll throw confetti. / Give away my Barbie doll / Give away my teddy / But don't give away my Alligator Spaghetti." Companion book: *Dinosaur Dinner (With a Slice of Alligator Pie)*, edited by Jack Prelutsky and illustrated by Debbie Tilley (Knopf, 1997).

Lesynski, Loris. *Dirty Dog Boogie*. Annick, 1999.

This inventive collection contains several poems that beg to be read aloud. Start a poetry session with "I Hate Poetry!" Topics include sock fluff, fidgeting, and mittens knit from the pet cat's leftover fur. Companion book: *Nothing Beats a Pizza* (Annick, 2001).

Lillegard, Dee. *Do Not Feed the Table*. Illustrated by Keiko Narahashi. Doubleday, 1993.

These funny, short poems revolved around the kitchen. The best one warns us not to use the spatula for swatting flies.

Livingston, Myra Cohn. *Lots of Limericks*. Margaret K. McElderry, 1991.

Several original and traditional limericks are grouped under a variety of topics. A sampler of a traditional favorite: "A tooter who tooted the flute / Tried to tutor two tooters to toot. / Said the two to the tutor / 'Is it harder to toot or / To tutor two tooters to toot?'"

Lobel, Arnold. *Whiskers and Rhymes*. Greenwillow, 1985.

Lobel created several new nursery rhymes such as "Boom, Boom," a poem about someone with excessively large feet; "Pickle Paste," a type of toothpaste that'll leave your teeth green; and "Clara, Little Curlylocks," a poem about a girl whose encounter with a lion straightens her hair.

McNaughton, Colin. *Wish You Were Here (And I Wasn't): A Book of Poems and Pictures for Globe Trotters*. Candlewick, 2000.

This collection of nonsense verse contains titles such as "Yet Another Poem to Send to Your Enemy," If You're Traveling in Transylvania," and "As I Went Walking," in which the narrator keeps encountering people who say nonsensical things. Companion books: *There's an Awful Lot of Weirdos in Our Neighborhood and Other Wickedly Funny Verse* (Candlewick, 1987); *Making Friends with Frankenstein: A Book of Monstrous Poems and Pictures* (Candlewick, 1994).

Merriam, Eve. *A Poem for a Pickle: Funnybone Verses*. Illustrated by Sheila Hamanaka. Morrow, 1989.

Highlights include poems about a girl who drops her glasses in molasses and a dog smart enough to know that the opposite of smooth is "rough."

Moss, Jeffrey. *The Butterfly Jar*. Illustrated by Chris Demarest. Bantam, 1989.

The former *Sesame Street* songwriter created a Shel Silverstein knockoff collection of poems, but some of the verses are quite good. The best is "Purple," in which the poet asks us to imagine what the world would be like if purple were the only color. Companion book: *The Other Side of the Door* (Bantam, 1991).

Prelutsky, Jack. *Awful Ogre's Awful Day*. Illustrated by Paul O. Zelinsky. Greenwillow, 2001.

A day in the life of an ogre, featuring his creepy-crawly pets, breakfast of Scream of Wheat, dancing and singing, and a nightmare of a place most of us would consider paradise.

Prelutsky, Jack. *For Laughing Out Loud: Poems to Tickle Your Funnybone*. Illustrated by Marjorie Priceman. Knopf, 1991.

Arguably the best collection of humor poetry by a variety of poets. The book appropriately opens with William Jay Smith's "Laughing Time" to set the mood. It couldn't end any better than the simple "Bursting" by Dorothy Aldis. Companion book: *For Laughing Out Louder: More Poems to Tickle Your Funnybone* (Knopf, 1995).

Prelutsky, Jack. *The New Kid on the Block*. Illustrated by James Stevenson. Greenwillow, 1984.

When Prelutsky is good, he's very funny. Otherwise, he's very repetitious and predictable. Luckily, this Shel Silverstein look-alike is mostly funny. The best poems include the title poem, "Dainty Dottie Dee," in which a compulsive house cleaner even cleans the garbage before throwing it out; "Dora Diller"; and "When Tillie Ate the Chili." Companion books: *Something Big Has Been Here* (Greenwillow, 1990); *A Pizza the Size of the Sun* (Greenwillow, 1996); *It's Raining Pigs and Noodles* (Greenwillow, 2000).

Prelutsky, Jack. *Poems of A. Nonny Mouse*. Illustrated by Henrik Drescher. Knopf, 1989.

Prelutsky collected several funny, anonymously written poems and accredited them to one A. Nonny Mouse. Companion book: *A. Nonny Mouse Writes Again!* (Knopf, 1993).

Rosen, Michael. *Walking the Bridge of Your Nose*. Illustrated by Chloe Cheese. Kingfisher, 1999.

Rosen has edited a large collection of tongue twisters, wordplay, riddle poems, and puns. Here's a tongue-twisting example: "'Night, night,

Knight,' said one knight / to the other knight the other night / 'Night, night, Knight.'"

Schwartz, Alvin. *And the Green Grass Grew All Around: Folk Poetry from Everyone*. Illustrations by Sue Truesdell. HarperCollins, 1992.

Here is a wealthy collection of poetry, street rhymes, folk songs, and parodies. Slip them in between the picture books in every story program. Here's an example of some of the sillier rhymes: "I love you, I love you / I love you lots. / My love for you / would fill all the pots / Buckets, pitchers, kettles and cans / The big washtub and both dishpans."

Shields, Carol Diggory. *Lunch Money and Other Poems About School*. Illustrated by Paul Meisel. Dutton, 1995.

This collection of school poems describes a dinosaur bus, a misfit named Eddie Edwards, the too many rules of recess, and a mixed-up school play.

Silverstein, Shel. *Where the Sidewalk Ends*. HarperCollins, 1974.

This is the touchstone book for all children's humorous poetry. Generations of school children know "Jimmy Jet and His TV Set," "True Story," "Boa Constrictor," "Sick," "Sarah Cynthia Sylvia Stout Would Not Take the Garbage Out," and many, many more. Companion books: *A Light in the Attic* (HarperCollins, 1981); *Falling Up* (HarperCollins, 1996).

Tripp, Wallace. *A Great Big Ugly Man Came Up and Tied His Horse to Me*. Little, Brown, 1973.

Tripp collected mostly short nonsense verse, including the traditional "A horse and a flea and three blind mice / Sat on a curbstone shooting dice / The horse he slipped and fell on the flea / The flea said, 'Whoops, there's a horse on me.'" Companion books: *Marguerite, Go Wash Your Feet* (Houghton Mifflin, 1985); *Rose's Are Red, Violet's Are Blue: And Other Silly Poems* (Little, Brown, 1999).

Viorst, Judith. *If I Were in Charge of the World and Other Worries*. Atheneum, 1981.

Yet another landmark book of children's poetry. The title poem begs for additional lines from the audience. Other classic poems include "Learning," Wicked Thoughts," "Some Things Don't Make Any Sense at All," ". . . And Then the Prince Knelt Down and Tried to Put the Glass

Slipper on Cinderella's Feet," and the amply titled "Thoughts on Getting Out of a Nice, Warm Bed in an Ice Cold House to Go to the Bathroom at Three O'Clock in the Morning." Companion book: *Sad Underwear and Other Complications: More Poems for Children and Their Parents* (Atheneum, 1995).

Westcott, Nadine Bernard. *Never Take a Pig to Lunch: And Other Poems About the Fun of Eating.* Orchard, 1994.

Westcott includes sixty poems that describe the joys and the sometimes disgusting low points of food. Highlights include "O Sliver of Liver" and "What You Don't Know About Food."

## ANTHOLOGIES AND FOLKLORE COLLECTIONS

Baltuck, Naomi. *Crazy Gibberish and Other Story Hour Stretches: From a Storyteller's Bag of Tricks.* Linnet, 1993.

This marvelous collection of audience participation stories and musical activities is highlighted by the funky verse of "Little Rap Riding Hood."

Brown, Marc. *Scared Silly!* Little, Brown, 1994.

This collection of original and traditional poems, jokes, stories, and songs features creepy and scary things. Highlights include Jack Prelutsky's "My Sister Is a Sissy," Ogden Nash's "The Python," and the traditional "One Hungry Monster."

Cole, Joanna, et al., eds. *Ready, Set, Read—and Laugh!* Doubleday, 1995.

This collection of humor is aimed at beginning readers. It contains riddles, rebuses, poems, and short stories featuring the likes of Amelia Bedelia, Morris and Boris, and Big Good and Little Goof. The highlight is the never-ending story "The Noisy Cow."

Goode, Diane. *Diane Goode's Book of Silly Stories and Songs.* Dutton, 1992.

The funniest of these traditional stories are "A Lion Went for a Walk," "Get Up and Bar the Door," "The Mistake," and "Bendemolena."

Hamilton, Martha, and Mitch Weiss, eds. *Noodlehead Stories: World Tales Kids Can Read and Tell.* August House, 2000.

The funniest stories include "Dead or Alive," in which a fool believes he's dead when he's not, and "The Farmer Who Was Easily Fooled," in which a thief tricks the farmer out of his donkey and his gold.

Holt, David, and Bill Mooney. *Spiders in the Hairdo: Modern Urban Legends.* August House, 1999.

This collection contains several funny legends and some more creepy ones that appeal to older children and teens.

Holt, David, and Bill Mooney, eds. *More Ready-to-Tell Tales from Around the World.* August House, 2000.

Among the several humor and non-humor stories are the hilarious "Why Armadillos Are Funny," adapted by Barbara McBride-Smith, and "The Barking Mouse," adapted by Antonio Sacre. Companion book: *Ready-to-Tell Tales: Sure-Fire Stories from America's Favorite Storytellers* (August House, 1994).

Lederer, Richard. *Pun and Games: Jokes, Riddles, Daffynitions, Tairy Fales, Rhymes, and More Wordplay for Kids.* Chicago Review Press, 1996.

One of the few sources that has some spoonerisms. This collection also contains fun knock-knock jokes and Tom Swifties. Companion book: *The Play of Words: Fun and Games for Language Lovers* (Pocket Books, 1991).

Lester, Julius. *The Tales of Uncle Remus: The Adventures of Brer Rabbit.* Illustrated by Jerry Pinkney. Dial, 1987.

Lester has written some hilarious retellings of the classic Brer Rabbit stories, many containing sly modern-day references. Highlights in the first volume include the classic "Brer Rabbit and the Tar Baby," and "Brer Rabbit and the Mosquitoes," a visual comedy for storytellers. Sequels: *More Tales of Uncle Remus: Further Adventures of Brer Rabbit, His Friends, Enemies, and Others* (Dial, 1988); *Further Tales of Uncle Remus: The Misadventures of Brer Rabbit, Brer Fox, Brer Wolf, the Doodang, and Other Creatures* (Dial, 1990); *The Last Tales of Uncle Remus* (Dial, 1994).

Low, Alice, ed. *Stories to Tell a 5-Year-Old.* Little, Brown, 1996.

While not all of the stories in the collection are humorous, there are several funny selections featuring Mrs. Piggle-Wiggle, Wayside School, Ramona Quimby, and several folktales such as "Lazy Jack" and "Clever Elsie." Companion book: *Stories to Tell a 6-Year-Old* (Little, Brown, 1997).

Pollack, Pamela, comp. *The Random House Book of Humor for Children.* Illustrated by Paul O. Zelinsky. Random, 1988.

This massive volume showcases selections from some of the funniest children's chapter books, such as Beverly Cleary's *Beezus and Ramona,* Robert Newton Peck's *Soup,* and Barbara Robinson's *The Best Christmas Pageant Ever.* It also contains works by humorists who don't write for children, but who young folks might find amusing. These writers include Bob and Ray, Shirley Jackson, Garrison Keillor, Sam Levenson, Patrick McManus, and Saki.

Tashjian, Virginia. *Juba This and Juba That: Story Hour Stretches for Large or Small Groups.* Little, Brown, 1969.

A classic collection of short audience participation stories and fillers. Companion book: *With a Deep Sea Smile: Story Hour Stretches for Large or Small Groups* (Little, Brown, 1974).

Van Laan, Nancy. *With a Whoop and a Holler: A Bushel of Lore from Way Down South.* Illustrated by Scott Cook. Atheneum, 1998.

This collection of poems, sayings, superstitions, songs, and stories features the likes of Brer Rabbit, Jack, and others. Try telling the tongue-twisting "Three Foots," featuring the "Foot," his ma "Foot-Foot," and his pa "Foot-Foot-Foot."

# THE FUNNIEST CHILDREN'S AUTHORS AND ILLUSTRATORS

Here they are. My inductees for the Robbie Hall of Fame for the Funniest Children's Authors and Illustrators. These eighteen book creators have proven themselves to be consistently funny. Long may we laugh at their creations: Hip-Hip, Ha-Ha!

## Beverly Cleary

Why does she make us laugh? Cleary's characters are unique, sometimes stubborn, but thoroughly realistic children. Their everyday challenges of growing up are told with a gentle writing style in which the humor sneaks up on the reader. Notable funny books: The Henry Huggins series, the

Ramona series, the Ralph S. Mouse series, the Jimmy and Janet picture books.

## Roald Dahl

Why does he make us laugh? Dahl's fantastic settings and unforgettable characters best demonstrate his irreverent humor as the little characters usually triumph over the evil, sometimes cloddish authority figures. His best-known books are probably *James and the Giant Peach* and *Charlie and the Chocolate Factory.* Notable funny books: *The BFG; The Twits; The Enormous Crocodile; George's Marvelous Medicine; Roald Dahl's Revolting Rhymes;* Dahl's autobiography, *Boy: Tales of Childhood.*

## Sid Fleischman

Why does he make us laugh? This teller of tall tales and wordplay also crafts action-packed adventures designed to keep the readers on the edge of their seats. Fleischman is perhaps best known for his Newbery Award winner *The Whipping Boy.* His McBroom series and his one-acre farm are some of the funniest tall tales ever written for children. Other notable funny books: *Jim Bridger's Alarm Clock and Other Tall Tales; Humbug Mountain; By the Great Horn Spoon!; Mr. Mysterious and Company;* Fleischman's autobiography, *The Abracadabra Kid: A Writer's Life.*

## Steven Kellogg

Why does he make us laugh? Kellogg's characters are full of life and energy. His detailed drawings are worth poring over. His tall tales bring some of America's favorite characters to life. Notable funny books: *Paul Bunyan; Pecos Bill; Sally Ann Thunder Ann Whirlwind Crockett;* the Pinkerton series; *Island of the Skog; The Mysterious Tadpole; Aster Aardvark's Alphabet Adventures.* Also see his illustrations for Trinka Hakes Noble's Jimmy's Boa series and D. M Schwartz's *How Much Is a Million?*

## James Marshall

Why does he make us laugh? Marshall's humor is irreverent and outrageous. His cartoon illustrations are very expressive, with funny details tucked in here and there. Notable funny books: The Fox series (as Edward Marshall); *Yummers; The Cut-Ups;* his renditions of popular folktales such as Red Riding Hood, The Three Pigs, Goldilocks and the Three Bears; and his illustrations for Harry Allard's Miss Nelson and The Stupids series.

## Robert Munsch

Why does he make us laugh? This storyteller/author's strengths lie in the tools of oral tradition: rhythm, repetition, and audience participation. His unique characters often appear in bizarre circumstances. Perhaps best known for *Love You Forever* and *The Paper Bag Princess,* his notable funny books include *Moira's Birthday; Mortimer; Thomas' Snowsuit; Mud Puddle; Stephanie's Ponytail.*

## Margie Palatini

Why does she make us laugh? Palatini is the queen of puns and master of alliteration. She sneaks in a lot of allusions to traditional rhymes and folktales. Read her books aloud and you'll have trouble getting though without laughing yourself. Notable funny books: *Piggie Pie; The Web Files; Earthquack!; Bedhead; Ding Dong Ding Dong; Moosetache; Tub-Boo-Hoo.*

## Barbara Park

Why does she make us laugh? Park has a great ear for funny dialogue. Her realistic characters are sometimes put in humorous situations. Park was funny long before her most popular character, Junie B. Jones, appeared on the scene. Other notable funny books: *Skinnybones; Operation: Dump the Chump; My Mother Got Married (and Other Disasters).*

## Dav Pilkey

Why does he make us laugh? Kids appreciate Pilkey's lowbrow (sometimes toilet) humor. His Captain Underpants books and the tag-along series featuring Super Diaper Baby are his best-known works. Other notable funny books: *Dogzilla; Dog Breath; The Hallo-wiener;* the Ricky Ricotta series; *The Dumb Bunnies* (written under his pseudonym—Sue Denim).

### Daniel Pinkwater

Why does he make us laugh? Like Dav Pilkey, Daniel Pinkwater isn't for everyone. Although their humor doesn't have universal appeal, they both have unique talents that make kids laugh. Pinkwater delights in creating intelligent misfits with weird names who find themselves in absurd situations. The puns and deadpan humor are frosting on the cake. Notable funny books: *Blue Moose; Lizard Music; Alan Mendelsohn, the Boy from Mars; Author's Day; Tooth-Gnasher Superflash; The Hoboken Chicken Emergency; Fat Men from Space; The Snarkout Boys and the Avocado of Death.*

### Louis Sachar

Why does he make us laugh? Sachar is the modern-day Lewis Carroll with his use of strange but carefully crafted logic in a sometimes absurd world. He is best known for *Holes*, a Newbery Award winner (and my all-time favorite children's book) and the Wayside School series. Other notable funny books: *There's a Boy in the Girls' Bathroom; Dogs Don't Tell Jokes;* the Marvin Redpost series.

### Jon Scieszka

Why does he make us laugh? Scieszka has revived the fractured fairy tale category with his many parodies and has proven his wit with The Time Warp Trio series. He is good at sneaking the unexpected, but funny, word or phrase in some books and then giving us some way-over-the-top actions. Notable funny books: *The True Story of the Three Little Pigs; The Frog Prince Continued; The Stinky Cheese Man and Other Fairly Stupid Tales; Math Curse; Squids Will Be Squids.*

### Dr. Seuss

Why does he make us laugh? His humor is timeless. He's been around for generations, and his books are still going strong. Most humor for children is somehow measured against Dr. Seuss. Don't analyze it; just enjoy it. Notable funny books: Pretty much everything he's created. Personal favorites: *The 500 Hats of Bartholomew Cubbins; Green Eggs and Ham; Horton Hatches the Egg; The Sneetches and Other Stories.*

### Shel Silverstein

Why does he make us laugh? Silverstein's irreverent verse showcases outrageous characters and situations. Like Dr. Seuss, Silverstein has had many imitators who don't reach the same quality of humor. Notable funny books: *Where the Sidewalk Ends; A Light in the Attic; Falling Up; A Giraffe and a Half; Lafcadio, the Lion Who Shot Back; The Missing Piece; Who Wants a Cheap Rhinoceros?*

### Janet Stevens

Why does she make us laugh? The expressions on Stevens's anthropomorphic animals are priceless (as are their clothes, when they wear any). Stevens specializes in retellings of both popular and little-known folklore. Her best work, *Tops and Bottoms*, won a Caldecott Honor (and should have won the big award). Notable funny books: *The Tortoise and the Hare; The Three Billy Goats Gruff; Coyote Steals the Blanket; Cook-a-Doodle-Doo; From Pictures to Words: A Book About Making a Book*; and illustrations for Eric Kimmel's Anansi series.

### James Stevenson

Why does he make us laugh? This prolific cartoonist conveys a lot of emotions and silliness in his deceptively simple line drawings. His Grandfather series contains some of the biggest whoppers around. Notable funny books: *Could Be Worse!* the Worst Person series; the Mud Flat series; and illustrations for Cynthia Rylant's Henry and Mudge series and Jack Prelutsky's poetry collections.

### Judith Viorst

Why does she make us laugh? In addition to having some of the longest book and poem titles in children's literature, Viorst points out the little nagging aspects of a child's life. By broadcasting them, she makes them funny. Notable funny books: *Alexander and the Terrible, Horrible, No Good, Very Bad Day; If I Were in Charge of the World and Other Worries; My Mama Says There Aren't Any Zombies, Ghosts, Vampires, Creatures, Demons, Monsters, Fiends, Goblins, or Things; Super-Completely and Totally the Messiest.*

## Nadine Bernard Westcott

Why does she make us laugh? This underrated illustrator has the most expressive human and animal faces. Each picture is filled with small, humorous details. Westcott specializes in making traditional songs, chants, and rhymes come to life. Notable funny books: *I Know an Old Lady Who Swallowed a Fly; The Lady with the Alligator Purse; There's a Hole in the Bucket; I've Been Working on the Railroad.*

# 9

## Two Last Treats

These two pieces, written in the style of humorist Dave Barry, applaud the patience and resourcefulness of children's librarians everywhere.

### UNATTENDED BR . . . UH, CHILDREN

Ever wonder how many of yards of tape are wound inside a children's video? I found out from an innovative and unattended three-year-old who unrolled the entire contents of a *Sesame Street* video and dragged it around the Children's Room before she and I came nose to nose some 890 feet (as the crow flies) from the video shelves. And my library director had the audacity to question my budget request for a nine-foot blinking neon sign that reads: ATTENTION PARENTS! YES, YOU! DON'T YOU DARE LEAVE THIS ROOM WITHOUT YOUR CHILD UNTIL HE OR SHE IS OLD ENOUGH TO QUALIFY FOR MEDICARE!

Yes, parents are forever depositing their hatchlings in the Children's Room and then sneaking past our staff despite the newly installed trip wires and attack dogs. They always say, "Oh, I'll just be gone a teeny-weeny second." Then they hide in the adult area and jot down the call numbers for all fiction and nonfiction titles that begin with the word "The." Meanwhile, junior is finding out how many issues of *Highlights* it takes to make the toilet overflow in the little boys' room.

What's wrong with these people? I have four kids myself and I know you don't take your eyes off of them for one nanosecond or the next thing you know, they'll be bungee-jumping from a pyramid constructed of *Where's Waldo?* books. Parents are getting desperate in their attempts to foist their offspring on our staff. "My God! What's that?" shouted a young mom the other day, pointing to a spot behind my shoulder. I looked behind me. A split second later, I cursed my gullibility and spun around. Too late. She was gone, leaving me with her six cherubic (a word meaning "inhabitants of Hades") children who were already constructing an obstacle course with the Story Room as the Fun House of Doom and the paperback stand as the Grand Champion Skateboard Ramp.

So, I'm hoping the library board will soon enact stronger . . . Excuse me. Some micro-twit's kids are trying to construct a flotilla in the fish tank out of the entire Harry Potter collection.

Oops! They're mine.

## STORY HOUR FOR THE UNAWARE

Army veterans dream about their war experiences. Paramedics remember their first accident scene. Librarians recover from their first Preschool Story Hour.

My name's Friday. I'm a librarian. The library has a million stories. Here's mine.

The call came in early. The children's librarian was out with the flu. The chief asked me to take over Preschool Story Hour. "No sweat," I replied. After all, how hard could it be?

At 10:30 A.M., I found myself facing several short library patrons. After stopping five of them from fighting, helping two more find Mommy, allowing six of them to get a drink from the water fountain, letting eight show me how many fingers old they were, and warning one not to mess with the light switch anymore, I got them seated.

"Where's the liberry lady?" asked a little boy. "Sick," I mumbled. "Now sit down and I'll read *Foo Foo the Flying Bunny*." "I have a bunny at home," said one child. "I can't see the pictures," said another. "I have to go to the bathroom," said a third child.

"Children! Sit down! Little girl, stop hitting the other children."

"I got some colors for my birthday," said one child. "I have that book at home," said another. "I have to go re-e-e-a-l-l bad!" said a third child.

"Okay," I said to the child waving her hand and hopping up and down. "You may go to the bathroom." "I gotta go, too!" cried several children. "Me, too! Me, too!" Most of the children headed for the Story Room entrance.

"Children!" I cried. "Everybody back to their seats! You'll have to wait until we finish the story." The children sat down and I began to read *Foo Foo the Flying Bunny*.

"Bunnies can't fly," said one child. "I got new panties," said another. "Are we done yet?" asked a third child. This continued for thirty minutes. We read four picture books, sang "The Eensy Weensy Spider" twice, and Hokey-Pokeyed eighteen times before I released the children back to their parents.

After slamming back a few aspirins, I asked the chief if I could knock off for the rest of the day. "Sure," she said. "As soon as you've finished afternoon Story Hour."

# Index

Authors, titles, subjects, and series are interfiled in one alphabet. Authors print in roman, titles in italics, subjects in bold, and series in quotes.

**Rob Reid** is a full-time consultant for the Indianhead Federated Library System in Eau Claire, Wisconsin, and a part-time instructor of Children's Literature and Literature for Adolescents at the University of Wisconsin, Eau Claire. Previously, he worked as a children's librarian for public libraries both in Wisconsin and Colorado. He has entertained children across the country for more than twenty years—and spends a lot of time on the road presenting workshops on children's library programming and as a "children's humorist" for school assemblies and library programs. Reid is the author of *Family Storytime* (ALA, 1999), *Children's Jukebox* (ALA, 1995), and the picture book *Wave Goodbye* (Lee & Low, 1996). He and his wife have four children, a golden retriever, and a mini-van they affectionately call Clifford the Big Red Van.